APPLE WATCH
USER GUIDE

An Easy, Step-By-Step Guide On Mastering The Usage Of Your New Apple Watch. Learn The Best Tips & Tricks, And Discover The Most Useful Secrets To Get The Max Out Of Your Device

BY
ETHAN COPSON

APPLE WATCH USER GUIDE © COPYRIGHT 2023

ALL RIGHTS RESERVED

ETHAN COPSON

Disclaimer

TABLE OF CONTENTS

TABLE OF CONTENTS

TABLE OF CONTENTS

INTRODUCTION

The Apple Watch is thought to be the company's most personalized product to date and makes daily tasks easier and more convenient for customers. Apple Watch is a smartwatch that you can wear. It lets you do a lot of things, like make phone calls, send text messages, and check your email. On April 24, 2015, Apple unveiled the Apple Watch.

The Apple Watch has to be linked to an iPhone 5 or later operating iOS 8.2 or above, and it must be within a 33-foot range for it to work. If both the watch and iPhone are connected to the same Wi-Fi network, they may also be connected through Bluetooth. Users may modify settings, organize applications, choose alerts, and download new apps from their iPhone using the Apple Watch iPhone app. Navigation on the Apple Watch is done by swiping and tapping, since the interface was created exclusively for the wrist. The watch's Digital Crown, a physical navigation dial that magnifies information, scrolls, and enters data, is situated on the side.

Users may begin a job on the Apple Watch and complete it on their iPhone thanks to the watch's Handoff feature. Users cannot, for instance, write emails on the watch, but they may ask the Siri digital assistant to do it, and it will send the work to the iPhone. (Siri is available on the Apple Watch, but she only responds to written commands; she cannot talk. The user may either speak "Hey Siri" or press and hold the Digital Crown to invoke Siri. Glances is another feature that corporate users will find handy. Glances are brief informational bursts that users may personalize and access by swiping up on the watch face. They are compiled from applications located on the user's iPhone.

With Watch Kit, developers may create new applications or alter those that already exist exclusively for the Apple Watch. The majority of Apple's existing applications, including messaging, are refactored iPhone apps; however, certain native apps, like Activity, Workout, and Camera Remote, have been created especially for the watch. A social networking app for Facebook and apps for hotels and airlines that let customers check in with their Apple Watches are examples of third-party applications. Evernote, which enables users to dictate information to their watches, and Salesforce1, which provides real-time information about client transactions, are examples of enterprise applications. Enterprise mobility management tools may be used by IT to send business emails straight to the Apple Watch.

The regular Apple Watch has an OLED display with an ambient light sensor to reduce glare and is available in two casing sizes, 38mm or 42mm. Apple provides two different watch models: the Apple Watch Sport, which has an extra-strong Ion-X glass display and a rubber band, and the luxury Apple Watch Edition, which has an 18-karat gold case. The battery life of an Apple Watch is 18 hours when in regular usage or 72 hours while operating only in Power Reserve mode. The watch face's bottom is secured by a circular magnetic charger that connects to the same charger as an iPhone using a USB connection.

CHAPTER ONE
THE LATEST WATCH OS 9

Watch OS 8 WAS released in September 2022, and it will be replaced by watch OS 9, the most recent version of the watch OS operating system that powers the Apple Watch. At the 2022 Worldwide Developers Conference in June, watch OS 9 was reveal to the world.

With an emphasis on improved health and fitness features, the watch OS 9 upgrade includes design enhancements, new watch faces, and new applications.

There are now four brand-new watch faces available. While Playtime showcases entertaining, animated, and anthropomorphic numbers produced in partnership with artist Joi Fulton, Lunar illustrates the link between the Gregorian calendar and numerous lunar calendars. Astronomy is an updated version of the original astronomy watch face with a remastered design and fresh star map and cloud data, while Metropolitan is a traditional type-driven watch face with a style that varies when the digital crown is rotated.

A number of current watch faces have also undergone design revisions. Modernized and improved complexities are provided for Utility, Simple, and Activity Analog, and backdrop color modification is included in Modular and X-Large. More photographs, such as those of kittens, pets, and landscapes, now have a depth effect thanks to the Portraits watch face. Additionally, the Focus mode function may now be tied to a particular watch face, allowing you to use a different watch face for "work" mode than "personal" Focus mode.

With the addition of sleep phases in watchOS 9, users can now monitor their sleep patterns and determine if they are in REM, Core, or Deep sleep. On an iPhone, the Health app offers a more detailed view of the data related to sleep stages.

Users of the Apple Watch can now manage and keep track of their prescription drugs, vitamins, and dietary supplements with the new Medications app. The application maintains track of prescriptions, reminds users when it's time to take them, and keeps an eye out for any potential drug interactions (U.S. only). Users may acquire additional details about their prescriptions by syncing data to the iPhone's Health app.

The Workout app has been upgraded so that users may switch between Workout Views using the Digital Crown. Additionally, a new feature allows users to design unique programs that can include work and recovery periods. Heart Rate Zones may be set up to track a workout's intensity, and additional notifications for pace, power, heart rate, and cadence can help users progress through exercises. Swimmers may now use a new automated kickboard identification stroke type, and a SWOLF score that combines stroke count with swimming time can be used to measure efficiency.

Running exercises in the Fitness app include additional information, and there is a new Multisport workout type for triathletes that can switch between swimming, riding, and running sessions. On widely utilized routes, runners have the opportunity to compete against the best or last finisher while also keeping track of their stride length, ground contact time, and vertical oscillation.

Apple has also included a new pacer feature that allows runners to choose a distance and target time for a run, and the Watch will calculate the speed needed to finish it. For all users, estimations of cardio recovery are now given after an outdoor walk, run, or hike even if the session doesn't reach its maximum intensity.

Users may get more out of HIIT, Cycling, Rowing, and Treadmill exercises with the support of on-screen advice and trainer coaching with watchOS' Fitness+ programs. Users of Fitness+ without an Apple TV may broadcast their workouts and meditations to compatible third-party TVs via AirPlay. This allows them to utilize the TVs without an Apple TV.

Apple has improved the atrial fibrillation (AFib) alerts in the ECG app and included a new AFib History feature. AFib sufferers may activate AFib History to measure their frequency and get more insight into their cardiac condition. This information can also be shared with medical experts.

You may change important information like the date, time, location, tags, and notes in the Reminders app. The Calendar app gives users access to List, Day, and Month views as well as the ability to add new events straight from the Apple Watch.

Apple updated the Apple Watch's notification system so that slender banners are less obtrusive when the device is being used. Additionally, Family Setup now includes the Home app, allowing children to operate smart home accessories from their wrists. With a double-pinch motion, users of the Apple Watch may do additional actions, such as beginning or stopping a workout, answering or finishing phone calls, and playing or pausing media.

The QWERTY keyboard on the Series 7 now supports more languages, including French, German, Japanese, Italian, Portuguese, and Spanish, and an accessibility feature called Apple Watch Mirroring enables users to manage their Apple Watch remotely from a connected iPhone via AirPlay.

Developers can now add share sheet support to their watchOS applications and link them with Apple TV thanks to a new CallKit API that enables calls from third-party VOIP apps to be answered on Apple Watch.

NEW APPLE WATCH APPEARANCE

LUNAR

The lunar watch face shows how the Gregorian calendar and the lunar calendars used by the Chinese, Islamic, and Hebrew civilizations relate to one another. With this watch face, you may utilize up to four complications.

PLAYTIME

Playtime is a vibrant, entertaining Apple Watch face with animated numerals that was created in collaboration with the artist Joi Fulton. The figures respond when you touch on them and the backdrop changes as you rotate the Digital Crown, animating the confetti. There are no problems; you may choose for a backdrop made of solid color or confetti.

METROPOLITAN

Turning the Digital Crown alters the look of the iconic Apple Watch face Metropolitan. When the wrist is lowered, specially created numerals spin to form tablets and alter in style and weight. The circular dial's colors may be changed and it can accommodate up to four complexities.

ASTRONOMY

Actually a remastered version of the original Astronomy watch face, Astronomy has a new star map and real-time cloud information for your area. The typeface may be changed, and the primary view can be set to the Earth, Moon, or Solar System. It supports two complexities, and you may fast-forward or rewind to watch the moon phase or planet's position on a different day by twisting the Digital Crown.

Watch Face Improvements:

Simple - New, updated complications.

Utility - New, updated complications.

Modular - Background color editing.

Activity Analog - New, updated complications.

Portraits - With the Portraits watch face, additional images—including ones of animals, dogs, and landscapes—have a depth effect.

X-Large - Background color editing.

SLEEP TRACKING

In watchOS 9, Apple significantly improved the built-in Sleep app on the Apple Watch by adding Sleep Stages. The Apple Watch can tell you how much time you spent throughout the night in REM, Core, or Deep sleep as well as how much time you were awake thanks to Sleep Stages.

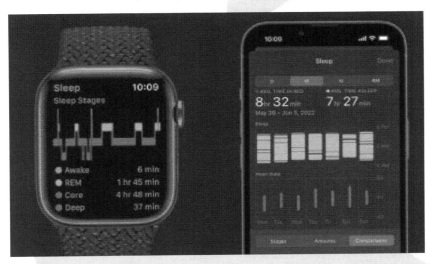

The Health app has charts that compare your heart rate and breathing rate as you sleep so you can evaluate how you're doing throughout the night.

MEDICATIONS APP

Along with a feature in the Health app on the iPhone, there is a new Medications app for the Apple Watch. You may add all of the prescription drugs, vitamins, and supplements you take, along with a schedule of when you should take them, to your iPhone.

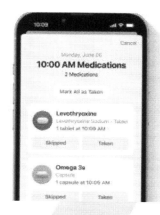

From there, you can set up your Apple Watch to remind you to take your meds and track your behavior by marking the times you remember to do so.

WORKOUT APP UPDATES

In watchOS 9, you may see new views of stats when working out that depend on the kind of exercise you're performing and include Activity rings, Power, Heart Rate Zones, and Elevation.

Heart rate zones make it possible for you to quickly gauge your degree of intensity. Depending on your heart rate, you may travel through several zones while you complete your exercise. You may manually establish training zones or the Apple Watch will compute them for you based on your unique health data.

Various work and rest periods may be added to workouts to accommodate different training philosophies, and the Apple Watch can provide notifications for pace, cadence, heart rate, and power so you can keep track of whatever statistic you need.

The new Running Form Metrics, which include stride length, ground contact time, and vertical oscillation, are all intended to help you understand how effectively you run. Apple will give feedback for running sessions to let you know whether you're on course to accomplish your objective.

Running Power, a measure of your effort when running, can also be calculated on the Apple Watch, and sessions like outdoor running have an improved workout summary.

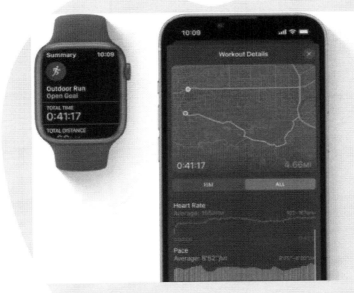

There are new multisport options for triathletes, and you can now choose to compete against your previous or greatest performance during Outdoor Run or Cycle sessions. Kickboard is a new stroke type that is supported by the Pool Swim workouts feature, and swimmers may monitor their SWOLF score for each set to gauge efficiency.

FITNESS+

On third-party televisions that are compatible, members to Apple Fitness+ who use AirPlay to watch their exercises may now see their real-time stats.

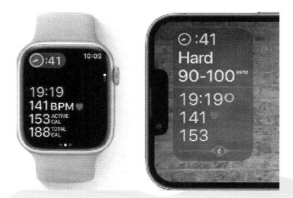

A new trainer callouts option has also been added to the service. Intensity Metrics will be mentioned by Apple Fitness+ teachers and will be shown on the screen as encouragement. The four levels of intensity are Easy, Moderate, Hard, and All Out.

In order to help customers manage their speed and get the most out of their exercises, trainers are now providing additional support with rowing, cycling, and treadmill workouts.

ECG ENHANCEMENTS

Atrial fibrillation (AFib), an abnormal heart rhythm that may signal major medical conditions, may be found using the ECG application on the Apple Watch.

Apple offers a new AFib History option that may monitor atrial fibrillation for anyone who have received a diagnosis. You can determine how often your heart suffers arrhythmias with AFib History, and you can also discover how things like sleep, activity, and weight might impact AFib.

OTHER NEW FUNCTIONS

Focus - Now that multiple watch faces may be assigned to distinct Focus modes, you can use a different watch face for each Focus.

Calendar-Events may be added to the calendar straight from the Apple Watch, and it's simple to go to certain days or weeks.

Dock - To make it simpler to return to background-running programs, they are given priority over other apps in the Dock.

Notification- Apple Watch alerts appear as inconspicuous banners while the device is being used. When the wrist is down and the Apple Watch is not in active mode, they are typical full-screen notifications.

Family Setup - Children who have their parents configure an Apple Watch now have access to the Wallet app's multiple digital keys, the Podcasts app, and the Home app.

Quick Actions - Depending on the app you're using, you can perform a double-pinch motion with Quick Actions to start a workout or capture a picture.

Calls may now be answered on the Apple Watch thanks to CallKit, a third-party VOIP software.

Apple Watch Mirroring: The Apple Watch Mirroring accessibility feature enables AirPlay-based control of the Apple Watch from an iPhone. Switch control and voice control are among the assistive features that are supported.

Maximum Battery Capacity Recalibration - According to the watchOS 9 release notes, Apple is introducing a new recalibration function for the Apple Watch Series

4 and Apple Watch Series 5. A more precise prediction of the maximum battery capacity will be produced by the recalibration.

COMPATIBILITY

Apple Watch Series 4 and beyond are compatible with watchOS 9, and watchOS 9 no longer supports the Apple Watch Series 3. Below is a complete list of compatible gadgets.

Apple Watch Series 8

Apple Watch Ultra

Apple Watch SE (second-generation)

Apple Watch Series 7

Apple Watch Series 6

Apple Watch SE (first-generation)

Apple Watch Series 5

Apple Watch Series 4

THE NEWEST APPLE WATCH

The eighth iteration of Apple's renowned series of smartwatches, the Apple Watch Series 8, will be released in 2022. The Apple Watch Series 7 from 2021 is mostly carried over into this year's edition, although it adds additional safety features, a temperature sensor, and the much better watchOS 9. The Apple Watch Ultra (the new premium model) is also included in the eighth installment of the Apple Watch series. With larger proportions, a tough (but stylish) titanium case, and a unique Wayfinder watch face, it magnifies everything that makes the Apple Watch 8 wonderful (which is aimed at hikers).

The two newest Apple smartwatches on the market right now are the Apple Watch 8 and Apple Watch Ultra, but the Apple Watch SE 2, which was released in September of this year, has a similarly long battery life, flawless software, and very thorough fitness monitoring. This chapter provides an overview of these three new models as well as a look back at prior Apple Watches that are no longer available by Apple.

WHAT IS THE NEWEST APPLE WATCH?

The most recent and cutting-edge Apple wristwatch currently on the market is the Apple Watch Ultra, which went on sale on September 23, 2022. It is closely followed by the Apple Watch Series 8 and Apple Watch SE (2022), all of which were unveiled on September 16, 2022. These devices replaced the Apple Watch Series 7 and Apple Watch SE (2020), with Apple eventually discontinuing these two models.

It's possible that the Apple Watch Series 8 is the ideal smartwatch. It offers improvements that allow it go beyond the Series 7 while looking fairly identical to it. In order to give users a more nuanced and finely grained overall picture of their general well-being. This technology also has the ability to identify automobile crashes, track different sleep cycles, and employ a new temperature sensor to monitor minor changes brought on by adjustments to a user's diet, exercise routine, and general health.

The rest of the elements that make the Apple Watch Series 7 such a great wearable are carried over, including a lot of the software and hardware functions. The Apple S8 has a 1.9-inch Retina OLED display that is lavish and detailed, at least as powerful as its predecessor, and watchOS 9 offers the same type of user-friendly interface that has made the Apple Watch the most well-liked product of its kind in the world.

Customers can chose from a range of hues (graphite, silver, and gold) and an ever-expanding array of bands because it is an Apple Watch. It goes without saying that connecting to your iPhone is simple and smooth, and the fitness and health monitoring tools are really unmatched, allowing users to establish goals and monitor their progress.

APPLE WATCH ULTRA

The Apple Watch Ultra is much different from the Apple Watch Series 8 if the former is the ideal wristwatch. It retains every element that makes the Series 8 such a unique smartwatch, but it now has a few high-end additions of its own. Its opulent titanium housing, which hides its greater proportions and display and offers some considerable durability, is perhaps most noticeable among them. Additionally, it features a battery that is substantially bigger and has a longer battery life than the

Series 9—roughly 36 hours as compared to 18. Additionally, it has a dual-frequency GPS that helps hikers track their whereabouts more accurately, making it somewhat more helpful as a fitness monitoring gadget than its less priced stablemate. Depth software for dives is also included.

The Apple Watch Ultra's particular capabilities don't end there; its proprietary Wayfinder watch face gives hikers and walkers information on elevation, slope, latitude, and longitude. The additional hardware button on the left side of the device may also be customized to function with certain applications in specific ways, making it easier to operate. It's also important to note that the Series 8's 1.92-inch Retina OLED display is brighter, reaching a maximum of 2,000 nits as opposed to 1,000.

Given how many more capabilities the Apple Watch Ultra can fit into such a compact space, doing so is nearly exhausting. To sum it up, there isn't truly a better smartwatch available right now.

APPLE WATCH SE (2022)

The Apple Watch SE (2022), Apple's Special Edition smartwatch's second iteration, offers excellent value. It boasts a much more potent S8 processor than the Series 8 and Apple Watch Ultra, although using the exact same design as the Apple Watch

Series 6 (and its predecessors). The battery life is comparable to that of the Series 8, but because it doesn't have the latter's always-on display, it frequently lasts slightly longer between charges.

Although the SE 2 lacks the new temperature sensor and the ECG monitor compared to the Series 8, it still allows customers to track their health and fitness in a sufficiently thorough manner. It offers alerts for things like excessively high or low heart rates, menstrual cycle monitoring, crash detection, fall and noise detection, and sleep tracking, as well as other things. Additionally, it can monitor a variety of exercises, showing the user's heart rate, active calorie burn, and other parameters while they work out.

The Apple Watch SE (2022) is perhaps more or less as excellent as the Apple Watch Ultra in terms of essential functionality, despite the fact that it may not have the same wow factor. In our opinion, it is a true winner since it is also lot less expensive.

DISCONTINUED MODELS OF APPLE WATCH SERIES

APPLE WATCH SERIES 7

Despite some minor cosmetic improvements, the Apple Watch Series 7 was very identical to the older Apple Watch Series 6. However, the Retina screen is 20% bigger and has a bezel that is 1.7mm, which is 40% smaller than that of earlier versions. The rounded edges of the casing are surrounded by a 2.5D screen that curves over the edge of the body and is coated with a thick, crack-resistant crystal. The bigger, always-on screen can show a complete keyboard and can accommodate 50% more text. When seen inside, the screen is 70% brighter than earlier versions, and the new IP6X dust resistance certification complements the WR50 water resistance rating of the earlier model.

Five colors, Midnight, Starlight, green, blue, and Product Red, are available for the aluminum edition, which supports new watch faces made for the bigger, curved screen. With case sizes of 41mm or 45mm, the Series 7 is also bigger, but it still works with all of the bands that have been on Apple Watches from the first model.

Like the S6, the Series 7 is powered by Apple's S7 SiP, a 64-bit dual-core CPU. It contains the same sensor array on the back that measures blood oxygen levels, heart rate, and can record an electrocardiogram (ECG). For exercises like cycling, there is a new fall detection function, and the Series 7 now tracks sleep respiratory rate thanks to watchOS 8.

The average battery life is 18 hours before a recharge is necessary. The battery of the Apple Watch Series 7 can be charged to 88% in only 45 minutes thanks to fast charging technology.

APPLE WATCH SE (2020)

The Apple Watch SE, to put it simply, is essentially the Apple Watch Series 6, with the exception of the absence of an electrocardiogram sensor, a blood-oxygen monitor, and the most recent S6 CPU. Otherwise, despite being less expensive, it's a very capable and strong smartwatch. Actually, the Apple Watch SE and Apple Watch 6 appear almost similar. It has a 1.78-inch Retina display with the same 326 pixel-per-inch density as the Series 6 model. Despite not having the choice of titanium or stainless steel, it also provides a large selection of bands and straps.

The Apple Watch SE is a fairly complete health and fitness tracker, despite the absence of the ECG and SpO2 sensors. Similar to the Apple Watch Series 6, you can use it to track your sleep and monitor your heart rate, and it also offers a ton of data for different types of exercises.

The SE's usage of the S5 CPU makes it incredibly speedy for the user experience as a whole. It integrates effortlessly with a broad variety of programs, from productivity-focused programs like Microsoft Teams to social networking tools like Twitter. The Digital Crown dial on the watchOS operating system is still simple to use and responsive, much as on prior Apple Watches.

The Apple Watch SE comes in two sizes, 40mm and 44mm, and for an additional $50, you can upgrade to a cellular-enabled model (letting you make telephone calls). Whichever choice you choose, you'll have one of the greatest smartwatches available.

APPLE WATCH SERIES 6

If you're fortunate, the greatest discontinued wristwatch available right now is the Apple Watch Series 6. It starts at $399 and has all the features you could ask for in a smartwatch. Its software is likely the smoothest on any watch now on the market, and its powerful Apple S6 processor can perform any work you'd need from a smartwatch. Its health and fitness monitoring is as thorough as anything else available.

Its base design has a lightweight aluminum frame, but you may pay extra money to upgrade to a more robust but slightly heavier stainless steel or titanium frame. The screen on the Apple Watch Series 6 makes the always-on display more visible and practical in the overwhelming majority of circumstances. The watch also has a blood oxygen (SpO2) sensor, which detects how much oxygen is in the blood and may help you get a general notion of how fast you recover from strenuous activity, for example. With its flawless software and battery life of around a day and a half with moderate use, it really is one of the finest fitness trackers available. It's no longer sold on the Apple website, but it is still offered by well-known retailers like Amazon, Target, and Walmart in both new and refurbished condition.

APPLE WATCH SERIES 5

The Apple Watch Series 5, which was released in September 2019, introduced the always-on display to the Apple Watch lineup for the first time and further solidified the Apple Watch's reputation for elegant software and demanding fitness-tracking capabilities.

While you won't be able to purchase it directly from Apple, a simple search reveals that it is still available via deep discounters like Dailysale as well as on websites like

Amazon and Best Buy in the form of used units. Even now, you may get a few new versions on Amazon.

APPLE WATCH SERIES 4

In our assessment of the Apple Watch Series 4 from 2018, we gave it a flawless score of 5 out of 5 and dubbed it "Apple's best hour in years." Even though it lacks the always-on display of the Series 5 and 6, it is still a fantastic smartwatch and performs much everything else you could expect from one. Its 1.78-inch Retina OLED screen is bright and clear, its appearance is (unsurprisingly) stunning, and its fitness tracking is consistently accurate. You'll also receive the most recent Apple Watch software updates since it is watchOS 7 compatible.

Even while you may get the Apple Watch Series 4 renewed or refurbished on Amazon, Best Buy, eBay, and Dailysale, it is currently rather difficult to locate a brand-new model online. Even now, you may get a few new versions on Amazon.

APPLE WATCH SERIES 3

It does seem strange to put the 2017 Apple Watch Series 3 in a chapter on the newest Apple Watches, to be sure. However, while discontinuing the Series 4, 5, and 6, Apple still offers the Apple Watch 3 as a budget option on its website. The Apple Watch Series 3 is still a very good wearable and was the first Apple Watch to include a 4G LTE cellular connection.

With its new starting price of $199, the Apple Watch 3 is now $80 and $200 less expensive than the base versions of the Apple Watch SE and Series 7, respectively. And for that price, you get a ton of goodies, including a 1.65-inch Retina OLED display with 303 ppi, the dual-core S3 CPU, a long battery life, a perfect software experience (it works with watchOS 7), and the usual assortment of practical health and fitness monitoring applications.

The Apple Watch Series 3 still has heart-rate monitoring and the GPS, accelerometer, gyroscope, and barometer you need to track various exercises, while lacking some of the more modern sensors seen in subsequent watch versions. It has essentially the same software features as more recent devices, such sleep monitoring and automatic hand-washing recognition, since it supports watchOS 8. Even while it may not be nearly as quick as the Series 7 (or SE), this smartwatch still performs better than many others in its class.

APPLE WATCH SERIES 2

We're really travelling back in time right now. The 2016 release of the Apple Watch Series 2 represented a significant improvement over its predecessor. The dual-core S2 CPU, a brighter OLED display, waterproofing (making it perfect for swimmers), and a built-in GPS sensor were also included. Together, these factors helped the wristwatch earn its place among legitimate health and fitness trackers, and the addition of watchOS 3 enhanced communications and included a variety of calming functions. However, the Series 2's rather limited battery life was a small drawback.

Nowadays, it would be quite difficult to locate a brand-new Apple Watch Series 2 for sale. It is no longer carried by retailers like Amazon and Best Buy, and Dailysale and even eBay only sell reconditioned units.

APPLE WATCH SERIES 1

If you're a historian of consumer tech, you may be interested in checking out the Apple Watch Series 1. Released back in 2015, it was Apple's first smartwatch, and while it lacks the refinement and power of its successors, it proved highly successful. You won't get as many fitness-tracking features as you would with the Series 6 or SE (or 5, 4, 6, or 3), but it is compatible up to watchOS 4, which provides support for a wider variety of workout types, as well as more watch faces, improved heart-rate visualizations, and a new Music app.

Unsurprisingly, you're not going to find this for sale new from Amazon, Walmart, or Best Buy. Instead, you'll have to go to eBay or Dailysale, where you'll find only pre-owned and refurbished models for sale.

The Apple Watch Series 1 could be something you want to look at if you're a consumer technology historian. It was Apple's first smartwatch, introduced back in 2015, and while lacking the sophistication and power of its predecessors, it was a huge hit. Compared to the Series 6 or SE (or the 5, 4, 6, or 3), you won't get as many fitness-tracking capabilities, but it is compatible with watchOS 4, which supports a broader range of exercise kinds and adds additional watch faces, enhanced heart-rate visualizations, and a new Music app.

Unsurprisingly, neither Amazon, Walmart, nor Best Buy will have this item available for purchase brand-new. You must instead visit Dailysale or eBay, where you can only buy used or reconditioned units.

The most recent Apple Watch is the Series 8, followed by the powerful Apple Watch Ultra and the affordable Apple Watch SE 2. The Series 8 maintains the majority of its features, including the same crisp screen, the same CPU, and almost all of the same fitness- and health-tracking functions, while the Ultra boasts the most features, the largest battery, and is simply the most eye-catching in terms of style and size. The SE 2 compares to the Series 8 in a similar fashion, with the cheaper model omitting an always-on display as well as the ECG and blood-oxygen monitors but including almost all other features.

Of fact, many of the smartwatches Apple has stopped making are still worth looking into if you can get them online, with the Series 7 and Series 8 being almost identical. Given the similarities between the most current Apple Watch models, such as the Series 7 or 6, you may want to wait another generation or two before upgrading.

CHAPTER TWO
FEATURES AND FUNCTIONS

What can I do on Apple Watch is a frequent question from prospective Apple Watch owners. I'll go through the main Apple Watch functions in this chapter, along with what an Apple Watch can accomplish with them. If you're considering purchasing this wristwatch and are looking for information about the main features and advantages of the Apple Watch, you've come to the right spot.

It would be clear that the Apple wristwatch writes a new chapter in wearable technology after reading over what an Apple Watch can achieve as detailed in the section. You may now communicate in novel ways directly from your wrist thanks to the introduction of an iOS-based user experience created especially for a smaller device. Wearable technology, including smart watches and smart glasses, is undeniably the next big thing after smartphones since it marks the next step in the development of the human-machine interaction.

WHAT CAN AN APPLE WATCH DO?

The Apple smartwatch isn't an independent gadget. It is a customized wristwatch designed to work in tandem with your iPhone and is intended to remain linked and connected to it so you may use the majority of the Apple Watch's features while wearing it. However, it also has some stand-alone capabilities. It is also designed to operate with Apple's new continuity features, which make it simple for users to switch between devices and complete activities.

Here are some of the main Apple Watch features and capabilities, along with some examples of what they may be used for.:

- Measure blood oxygen level (series 6)
- GPS tracking Heart rate monitoring;
- ECG monitoring (on Watch Series 4, 5, and 6 only);
- of workouts (on GPS versions);
- Get messages and notifications on the wrist;
- Answer calls on your wrist;
- Make calls and receive messages away from your phone (LTE versions with a data plan);
- Control Music;
- Tell the time;
- Turn-by-turn navigation;
- Fitness tracking;
- Workout tracking;
- Siri commands – alarms, timers, reminders;
- Display tickets and boarding passes;

Let's examine how an Apple Watch functions now that we have seen what it can do with its capabilities.

HOW DOES AN APPLE WATCH WORK?

Your connected iPhone and Apple Watch can interact over WiFi and Bluetooth. The "Digital Crown" must be stated first in order to explain how an Apple Watch functions.

The side-mounted scroll-wheel Digital Crown on the Apple Watch offers a novel method to seamlessly scroll, zoom, and navigate without disturbing the screen. The Digital Crown is now much more handy for sending smart messages since it serves as a Home button (to return to the home screen) and makes it simple to access built-in Siri. The "Taptic Engine" of the Apple Watch generates "haptic" input when you get alerts, alarms, and other messages. You get a tangible feeling on the wrist that is clearly different for each kind of interaction whenever you receive an alert or notification, as well as when you conduct actions like spinning the Digital Crown or pushing down on the display. It should be evident from the information provided above how an Apple Watch performs.

Before we get into the specifics of the Apple Watch's main features, let's take a short look at some of its essential characteristics.

APPLE WATCH FEATURES AND SPECIFICATIONS

Key specifications of Apple Watch:

- Features WiFi 802.11b/g and Bluetooth 4.0 to pair with iPhone;

- Available sizes: 38mm and 42mm (1.5 and 1.7 inches);

- 200 to 250 mAh battery – 18 hours battery life and MagSafe charging;

- Wireless Charging 512MB RAM;

- 4GB internal storage for music;

- Bio-metric functionality;

- Integration with the iPhone, iPad, and Mac;

- Apple Watch requires iPhone 5, iPhone 5c, iPhone 5s, iPhone 6, or iPhone 6 Plus running iOS 8.2. or later;

- NFC-enabled Apple Pay feature;

- Use Skin Contact for Apple Pay Security;

- Force Touch Retina touchscreen display with sapphire glass or Ion-X glass cover, depending on the model;

- A heart rate sensor, accelerometer, gyroscope, ambient light sensor, and two microphones for improved call quality are other features of an Apple Watch.

Although Apple has released a number of its own applications for the Apple Watch, it has also made the platform available to other app creators.

APPLE WRIST WATCH VERSIONS

Three variations of the Apple watch have been released: the Apple Watch, Apple Watch Sport, and Apple Watch Edition. With a variety of watch faces and leather, metal, and plastic bands, it is completely personalizable.

The original model, known as the "Apple Watch," is the only one that offers a polished stainless steel casing and the options of steel or space black finishes. The Ion-X glass screen on the second model, the "Apple Watch Sport," is lightweight, scratch- and impact-resistant. Aluminum that has been anodised makes up its body. The third model, called "Apple Watch Edition," was constructed of 18-karat rose or yellow gold but has subsequently been replaced with a ceramic version. Since ceramic is one of the world's toughest materials and is more than four times as durable as stainless steel, the Apple Watch Edition is very scratch-resistant.

Each of the three models is also available in two sizes, so users may choose the one that suits their wrists the best.

WHAT DOES AN APPLE WATCH DO USING ITS KEY FEATURES

While other Apple Watch capabilities seem to be more insignificant, there are a few very great Apple Watch activities that can be performed directly from your wrist. See what the Apple Watch can achieve below utilizing its main functions.:

NAVIGATING THE WATCH SCREEN

The iWatch's "Digital Crown," which facilitates navigating the tiny watch screen, is one of the device's most notable and nicest features. The right edge of the watch has a knob called the Digital Crown that serves as the home button. You may cycle through interface choices or zoom into programs by rotating it while pressing it to return to the home screen.

What can the Digital Crown on an Apple Watch do? To reach the home screen from your watch face, just push the Digital Crown. To switch between your two most recently launched applications, double-press the Digital Crown after pressing it once to exit an app. As an alternative to saying "Hey Siri," the device may alternatively be held to manually activate Siri.

TELL TIME ACCURATELY

Apple watches are very accurate at keeping time. Using the internet, the gadget will sync to the local time within 50 milliseconds. Travelers will find the watch to be of great use since it can also be used as a stopwatch, timer, alarm clock, and world clock. When you change time zones, Apple Watch does it automatically. When

DST kicks in, Apple Watch just adjusts to the new time. As a result, you'll never have to do it yourself.

HOW TO USE APPLE WATCH TO READ THE TIME

Simply elevate your wrist to see the time, and your Apple Watch should do the same, just like a conventional wristwatch.

CONTROL MUSIC

The Apple Watch's ability to manage music on your iPhone, iPad, or computer is one of its most well-liked functions. Additionally, it can playback music independently nearly as well as any iPod ever could and store up to 2GB locally. Because of this capability, the Apple Watch is ideal for runners. The playing of music on your iPhone, both from iTunes and locally saved music, may also be controlled by the Apple Watch. Whether you're at your workplace or somewhere else, if your iPhone is streaming to AirPlay-capable speakers, you can manage anything from your wrist.

NOTIFICATIONS & ALERTS

One of the most crucial advantages of an Apple Watch is its ability to keep you linked to your alerts without requiring you to always have your iPhone close by. With the Apple wristwatch, all of your alerts are at your fingertips, just as if someone were standing next to you and tapping your wrist each time one came in. You may enable a Notification Indicator, which will show a red dot on your watch face if you have unread notifications, to make sure you don't miss any alerts. Lifting your arm is all it takes to see a notice. Swiping down from the watch face will bring up the Notification Center. Despite the fact that we may not want to delete vital messages or alerts, we also don't want you to become lost in a sea of unwanted ones. You have two choices if you find yourself in a position like this: manually dismiss each notice by swiping down on it or scrolling to the bottom of it, or dismiss all alerts at once. Simply firmly press the Erase All button in the Notification Center to instantly clear all of your alerts. This will remove all alerts from your iPhone and Apple Watch.

Scroll to the bottom of the notice to find the response button, then press it to take the desired action. Your iPhone receives alerts instead of your Apple Watch when you lock it or choose "Do Not Disturb."

The notifications on your Apple smartwatch are really configured by default to mimic the settings on your iPhone, so any app for which you have enabled alerts on your iPhone will likewise display notifications on your Apple wristwatch. You may personalize the Apple Watch's alerts for built-in applications by doing the following:

On your iPhone, launch the Watch app, choose My Watch, and then select Notifications;

Tap an app;

Tap Mirror my iPhone to have the app's notification settings match those on your iPhone. Tap Custom to utilize customized notification settings especially for your Apple Watch.

Some Apple applications, including as Calendar, Mail, and Messages, provide a few extra features that may be changed. Make sure the notification you want to modify is already turned on on your iPhone.

REMOTE CONTROL FUNCTIONS

One of the most crucial functions for the Apple Watch is remote control. Your Apple Watch will serve as a remote control for your gadgets, so you may never have to get up from your couch again. With only a flick of your wrist, you can browse your Apple TV menu, scroll through your iPhone or iTunes music collection, activate "Do Not Disturb" and "Airplane" mode on your phone, and switch on or off your smart home lighting.

USING SIRI

One of the key features of the Apple Watch is Siri. The voice-activated digital assistant of Apple is a significant component of the Apple watch. Due to Siri's integration with Apple's wristwatch, you can do many of your favorite voice command chores without taking your iPhone out of your pocket, such as dictating a message, requesting to see your upcoming events, asking a question, and getting a response. On your phone, Apple's digital assistant performs all of its capabilities, including message sending and site searches.

Even if Apple Watch Siri isn't nearly as feature-rich as iPhone Siri, it still has a ton of capabilities. This Apple Watch function works just as well as Siri on the iPhone to switch items on and off. You may ask Siri to switch on or off Airplane mode, Bluetooth, Bluetooth Low Energy, and even accessibility capabilities like Voice-over.

HOW TO USE SIRI ON THE APPLE WRISTWATCH

Either lift your wrist and say, "Hey Siri," or press and hold the Digital Crown to invoke Siri. Unlike Siri on the iPhone, Siri on the Apple watch responds to your orders through text rather than speech. Saying the phrase "Hey Siri, what type of things can I ask you?" will bring up a long list of the things that the Apple Watch's Siri can perform. The lengthy list contains all of the tasks that Siri is capable of carrying out, including as alarm setting, app launching, call making, and message sending. Weather, maps, music players, sports results, market prices, fundamental Q&A information, etc. Additionally, each item has a list of phrases you may use to activate each function, with examples.

TRACK HEALTH AND FITNESS

One of the most practical Apple Watch functionalities is the ability to measure your health and fitness levels. The Apple iWatch is a fantastic fitness and wellness gadget that inspires you to move more. One of the great Apple Watch applications is called Activity. It tracks all of your activity throughout the day, including standing, moving, and jogging, and it reminds you to get up when you've been sitting motionless for too long. How is this achieved with the Apple Watch?

The app does this by allowing you to set and monitor three daily goals: spend less time sitting down (your goal is to stand up for at least one minute during each of at least 12 different hours), move more (measured in terms of calories burned), and document 30 minutes of vigorous exercise each day. Goals may be specified, and the app displays your progress on rings that fill up as you come closer to your objectives. While the built-in exercise app provides real-time data like as distance traveled and calories burnt and allows you to set objectives for each workout, the app records your everyday activities and retains that information over time. With daily summary displaying your step count and heart rate, an integrated heart-rate sensor monitors your heart health. According to Apple, the Apple Watch learns to know you over time much as a personal trainer would.

Press the Digital Crown and touch the symbol that resembles three rings in blue, green, and red to keep track of your daily activities. Your daily activity objectives are represented by the three rings: standing, exercise (green for movement), and movement (red for calorie count) (blue, with a target of standing once per hour). The "activity" symbol will always be shown on your watch face if you use the Siri watch face.

MONITOR YOUR EXERCISE

Your daily exercise may also be tracked by the Apple Watch. Look for the green emblem with the picture of a runner by pressing the Digital Crown. You may select the exercise that is right for your activity by tapping the symbol and scrolling through the list. Options range from yoga to high-intensity interval training.

The specific tracking changes, such as the time goal and your calorie count, are opened when you tap the three dots in the top right corner of the screen.

MEASURE YOUR HEART RATE

Another one of the Apple Watch's most crucial features is heart rate monitoring. Let's now examine how the Apple Watch measures your heart rate.

Make sure the Apple Watch is securely yet pleasantly fastened to your wrist if you want to manually measure your heart rate. Simply tap the Digital Crown and look for the heart symbol after that. When you tap the symbol, the watch begins taking your heart rate right away. Your heart rate history is shown on a graph at the top of the screen. You may separate your heart rate data into segments when walking and resting by turning the Digital Crown to see various displays.

According to reports, the Apple iWatch and the Cardiogram app may identify atrial fibrillation, one of the most prevalent cardiac arrhythmias. Additionally, the accuracy rate is rather good, making it trustworthy in addition to easy.

NAVIGATE AROUND WITH THE HELP OF APPLE MAPS

With the aid of Apple Maps, Apple Watch can also display your present position, turn-by-turn instructions, and the estimated time it will take you to get there. The haptic feedback is perhaps the most intriguing and distinctive aspect of Apple Maps on the wrist.

How does this Map application function with the Apple Watch? Once you've built up your walking path, the watch will effectively buzz when it's time to turn right or left (a different sensation for each direction). This enables users to acquire directions without even glancing at their wristwatches, enhancing roadway safety.

The Maps app lets you go about as well. Swiping up will bring up your Maps Glance, which you can access quickly. However, if you want to interact with it, you'll need to press on it to launch the full Maps app. The Maps app will show your current position after it has been launched. Using your fingertips or the Digital Crown, you may zoom in and out. Simply push hard on the screen and choose "Search" to look up a place. The Apple Watch will provide all pertinent information about the location, including contact details, hours of operation, and reviews, after you've searched for your selected destination. After choosing your preferred mode of transportation (walking or driving), with an estimated travel time next to each, press "Start" to begin turn-by-turn guidance.

APPLE PAY

One of the most helpful features of Apple Watches is Apple Pay, which offers a quick, simple, and secure method to make payments with your Apple wearable. Apple Watch makes this useful feature available to users of iPhone 5 and later. Users of the Apple Pay payment method may stop using their plastic cards. There is no need to look around for your credit card, provide ID, and sign a receipt anymore. Even simpler than taking out your phone, Apple Watch supports the new

NFC-enabled Apple Pay technology incorporated into the iPhone. You just need to touch your watch on the reader once to complete the transaction.

HOW TO USE IWATCH TO MAKE PAYMENTS THROUGH APPLE PAY

You just need to double-click the side button on your iPhone's NFC-capable Apple Pay feature, choose the card you wish to use, then hold the Apple Watch face up to a payment terminal or scanner. Your money has been received when you hear a beep and feel "a soft pulse."

PASSBOOK INTEGRATION

When traveling, you can speed through airport security thanks to Passbook on the Apple Watch. You won't need to reach for your phone to access your airline tickets, boarding permits, and loyalty cards. The app will also notify you when you enter a location where your discount or loyalty cards may be utilized.

UNLOCK HOTEL ROOM

It will be simpler to access your hotel room with a touch on your Apple Watch than to get your room key out of your wallet thanks to a software that turns the watch into a room key. It's unclear, however, if this will function with all of the group's properties. In certain hotels, including Sheraton, W Hotels, Westin, and others run by Starwood Hotels, you may use your Apple Watch as your room key. But if many more hotels eventually follow suit, you shouldn't be shocked.

ACTIVATION LOCK

One of Apple Watch's new features is Activation Lock. This iWatch functionality was only just released by Apple for security concerns. Your iCloud Apple ID and password must be entered in order to activate your Apple Watch since this secures it to your account and prevents unauthorized access in the event of theft. However, utilizing this function is not required.

CHANGE THE APPLE WATCH FACE.

The Apple Wrist Watch's ability to be customized is one of its main selling factors. Simply force touch the iWatch face to switch the watch face. You will then be sent to a menu where you may swipe left or right to choose from a number of watch faces, some of which are conventional and others which are not. Simply touch the watch face you want to choose after you've discovered it.

Although Apple does not let developers to make watch faces for the Apple Watch, you may still customize your watch face with some unique designs. On a "Tumblr" blog called "AppleFaces," you may download a variety of designs that are the right size to be utilized as Watch faces. For them to show up on your Watch, you must first download them into your iPhone.

MAKE PHONE CALLS

The Apple Watch offers a number of call-making options. By pushing the side button just below the Digital Crown, you may access your favorite contacts and choose the person you wish to call if they are on your list of favorites. To make a call from your Apple Watch after choosing the recipient, just press the Phone icon in the lower left-hand corner of the screen.

The Phone app, which is accessible from the home screen, allows you to make calls from the Apple Watch as well. Similar to the iPhone app, the Phone app allows you to start a call from your Apple Watch by selecting a contact from the list of categories when it is opened.

Additionally, you may use your Apple Watch as a tiny Bluetooth loudspeaker to answer calls. Your Apple watch will ring in addition to your iPhone when you get a call. If you want to silence this, put your hand over the screen. If you want to take the call on your Watch, hit the green symbol.

Using the Digital Crown, scroll down to "Answer on iPhone" if you don't want to answer the call on your watch. When you do this, the call is transferred to your iPhone and the other party is placed on hold until you unlock it and answer it.

HOW TO CHARGE THE DEVICE

To power the gadget Apple's MagSafe technology and inductive charging are combined in the special charging mechanism that comes with the iWatch. Simply insert the connection close to the watch's back, where magnets make it immediately snap into place.

WHAT ARE THE APPLE WATCH'S BIGGEST ADVANTAGES?

The main advantages of Apple Watch are as follows:

1. Even if a senior family member doesn't own an iPhone, Apple Watch is still an excellent option for them thanks to features like fall detection, emergency SOS, and high and low heart rate alerts;

2. You may easily remain in touch with your family by calling, messaging, and sharing your whereabouts.

Is Facetime available on Apple Watch?

On your Apple Watch, you can make Facetime Audio calls, yes. Finding a quiet area to make the call is preferable. Though audio quality has significantly increased in more recent Apple Watch models, it still falls short of an iPhone call in terms of quality. It's simple to make a Facetime call with the Apple Watch.

Can you text on Apple Watch?

On your Apple Watch, you can text. On your Apple Watch, you may read, respond, and send new text messages.

Does Apple Watch have a camera?

No, the Apple Watch lacks a camera. However, after seeing the image captured by your iPhone camera, you may use it as a remote to shoot pictures.

How distant can an iPhone be from an Apple Watch?

Although the typical Bluetooth range is between 10 and 15 meters, your Apple Watch will keep in touch with your iPhone wherever you are in the home where that network is covered when you're linked to a Wi-Fi network.

Is the Apple Watch waterproof?

Apple rates the Apple Watch as highly water resistant but does not advertise it as waterproof. While Apple advises against exposing the Watch to soaps, shampoos, conditioners, and fragrances because they may harm the device's water seals and acoustic membranes, it is OK to wear the watch in the rain or while taking a shower.

CHAPTER THREE
HOW TO SET UP YOUR APPLE WATCH

Do you need help configuring your Apple Watch? Even if you've already taken your new wristwatch out of the box, you still need to correctly set up your Apple Watch before you can respond to messages or interact with Siri on your wrist.

The Apple Watch is the greatest smartwatch money can buy for a variety of reasons. It works well as a communications and fitness tracker in daily life. With features for a variety of situations, it is also great for safety.

You can anticipate a simple user experience whether you have purchased an Apple Watch Series 8, Apple Watch SE (2022), or even the upcoming Apple Watch Ultra. But in order to have your Apple Watch operating the way you want, you'll need to know how to set it up.

Here are a few easy steps to setting up your Apple Watch.

How to configure an Apple Watch

1. On your iPhone, launch the Apple Watch app.

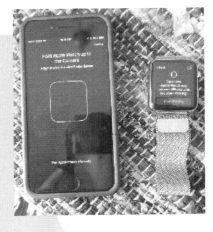

2. Select Start Pairing.

3. Pair your Apple Watch with your iPhone. So that your phone's camera can see the watch's pattern, hold the watch up to it. A 6-digit code that shows on the watch will be required to be entered when you choose "Pair Apple Watch Manually" and touch the watch's name in the Apple Watch app.

4. "Set Up as New Apple Watch" may be found in the Apple Watch app on your iPhone.

5. Choose the wrist that best suits you, left or right. Additionally, you'll be prompted to choose whose side you want the digital crown to belong to.

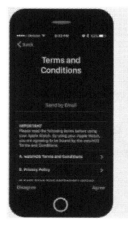

6. Choose Agree on the Terms and Conditions page.

7. Log in your Apple ID.

8. Select OK when asked about Location Services, Siri, or Diagnostics.

9. For your watch, create a 4-digit passcode.

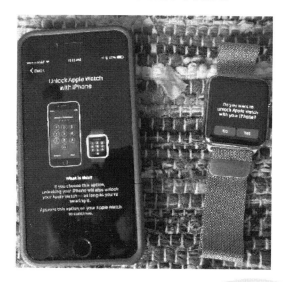

10. Decide whether you want to use your iPhone to unlock the Apple Watch. On the display of your watch, click Yes or No.

11. Set up Emergency SOS and Apple Pay (optional). While Emergency SOS, a new feature in watchOS 3, allows you to summon emergency services and send an alert to certain contacts, Apple Pay enables you to use your watch to make mobile payments. You may skip this step and configure these services at a later time.

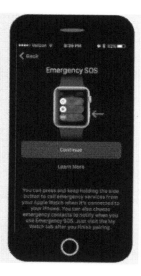

12. Add applications to your Apple Watch. When asked, choose Install All to instantly begin downloading the Apple Watch versions of the applications that are currently installed on your iPhone, or choose Later to choose just one.

13. Now, your iPhone and Apple Watch will begin synchronizing. As soon as the synchronizing is finished, you may start using the device.

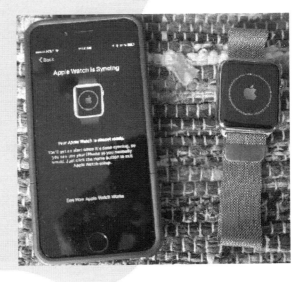

HOW TO PERSONALIZE YOUR APPLE WATCH

How to personalize your Apple Watch with the settings function is covered in this chapter. For all Apple Watch models, the steps are applicable.

HOW TO ACCESS APPLE WATCH SETTINGS

The watch has a number of standard capabilities that may be managed via its Settings interface even without third-party applications.

To access Settings, touch the gray and white gear icon after pressing the Digital Crown to return to the Home screen. In the order they appear on the device, the options for this interface are presented and explored below.

You may experiment with additional commands and features as you choose each option.

Some menu choices may seem different depending on the watch model you have, but the procedures for altering settings are essentially the same on all Apple Watches.

CHANGE THE TIME

You can use this feature to advance the time shown on your watch face by up to 60 minutes by using the wheel and the corresponding Set button. If you frequently come late for meetings or anything else, this self-inflicted psychological ruse may be exactly what you need to be where you need to be a few minutes early or on time.

The value utilized by your watch's alerts, notifications, and alarms are unaffected by this; just the time shown on the face is. These processes make use of real time.

SET YOUR WATCH TO AIRPLANE MODE

There is just one button in this area, which toggles Airplane Mode on and off. All wireless transmission on the watch, including Wi-Fi, Bluetooth, and cellular connections like phone calls and data, is turned off when it is engaged.

When in flight or in any other scenario when you'd prefer to disable all forms of communication without turning off your smartphone, Airplane Mode comes in useful.

An orange aircraft symbol appears at the top of the watch screen when it is activated.

MODIFY THE BLUETOOTH OPTION

You may link your Apple Watch with Bluetooth-enabled devices like speakers or headphones. This screen displays a list of all Bluetooth devices that are connected to your watch, in pairing mode, and nearby. A Bluetooth device may be linked by choosing its appropriate name and, if necessary, inputting a key or pin number.

One half of the Bluetooth screen is for ordinary devices, while the other is for devices designed specifically for recording your health statistics. Monitoring such statistics, such as your heart rate and daily activities, is one frequently utilized function of the Apple Watch.

Select the information icon next to the name of the Bluetooth pairing, then hit Forget Device to end the connection.

USE THE DO NOT DISTURB FUNCTION

Only an on/off button is included in this area. All calls, texts, and other notifications on the watch are muted while in Do Not Disturb mode. The Control Center, which can be accessed by sliding up while looking at the watch face and hitting the half-moon symbol, may also be used to turn this on and off.

This symbol always appears towards the top of the screen while it is active.

GENERAL SETTINGS ON THE APPLE WATCH

Each of the subsections in the General settings section is described below.

ABOUT

The About section displays information about the device, including its name, the quantity of music, photos, and applications, original capacity (in GB), available capacity, watchOS version, model number, serial number, MAC address, Bluetooth address, and SEID.

Although often ignored, this section might be helpful for resolving a watch or external connection issue. You may use it to calculate how much space is still available for applications, pictures, and music files.

ORIENTATION

Using the Orientation options, you can decide which arm you wish to wear your Apple Watch on and which side the Digital Crown (also known as the Home Button) is on.

To match the arm you select, tap Left or Right in the Wrist heading. Touch Left under the Digital Crown category to make the device function as it should if you turned your phone such that the Home button is on the left side.

WAKE SCREEN

When the Apple Watch isn't being used, its display automatically turns off in order to save battery life. You have control over how your watch wakes up from its power-saving sleep and what occurs when it does thanks to the several options included in the Wake Screen section.

The Wake Screen on Wrist Raise button, which is located towards the top of the screen, is turned on by default. Raising your wrist activates the watch display, which comes on while you're moving. Tap the button until it becomes gray instead of green to turn off the function.

The On Screen Raise Show Last App setting, located below this button, offers the following choices:

Only displays an app when the wrist is raised while the session is still in progress.

The default setting displays a recently used app that was utilized within the last two minutes.

When you lift your wrist, an app that was last used within an hour will be shown.

Every time your wrist is raised, the most recent app that was open is shown.

How long the display is active once a user taps its face is determined by the last Wake Screen option, On Tap. Additionally, it offers the two choices of Wake for 70 seconds and Wake for 15 seconds (the default).

WRIST DETECTION

When your watch is not on your wrist, this security-focused mode can tell. When you try to access its interface, the gadget instantly locks and asks for your password.

You may turn off this function by touching the corresponding button once, albeit doing so is not advised.

NIGHTSTAND MODE

When not on your wrist, the Apple Watch may be used as a convenient bedside alarm clock by lying gently on its side and plugged into the usual charger.

The date, time, and any alarms you may have set are all horizontally shown in Nightstand Mode, which is on by default. With each passing minute until your alarm goes off, the watch display glows a little brighter in an effort to lull you to sleep.

Make one selection of the button at the top of this section so that it becomes gray to turn off Nightstand Mode.

ACCESSIBILITY

The accessibility features of the watch allow users who may be blind or deaf to get the most out of their gadget.

The accessibility-related features listed below must all be manually enabled using this settings interface since they are all by default deactivated.

VoiceOver: Turns on a built-in screen reader that walks you through the watch's key capabilities and its pre-installed applications including Calendar, Mail, and Messages. More than twenty different languages are supported by the VoiceOver reader.

Zoom: This feature allows for a fifteen-fold virtual magnification of the display.

Reduce Motion: When enabled, the movement of the Home screen icons and other significant screen components is streamlined and closely associated with your navigational motions.

All on/off buttons should have a label that clearly indicates whether the corresponding setting or feature is presently active.

SIRI

Siri is accessible on the Apple Watch to act as a wearable virtual personal assistant, just as it is on Apple's other portable devices like the iPad and iPhone. The primary distinction is that, while Siri is voice-activated on the watch, it answers to your commands by sending you text messages rather than speaking to you like it would on a phone or tablet.

Use one of the aforementioned techniques to awaken the watch display, then say Hey Siri to activate Siri. Holding down the Digital Crown (Home) button until the phrase "What can I assist you with?" appears can also bring up the Siri interface.

One option in the Siri settings area toggles the feature's availability on the watch. By touching this button once, you may turn it off from its enabled state.

REGULATORY

There are no programmable parameters in the Regulatory area. Instead, it provides facts on the device, such as the model number, FCC ID, and information regarding regional compliance.

RESET

There is just one button, but it is most likely the most powerful, under the Reset area of the Watch settings screen. By choosing the option titled "Erase All Content and Settings," the phone is returned to its factory settings. Activation Lock won't be eliminated, however. If you want to get rid of it, you must unpair the watch.

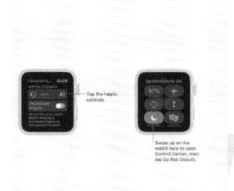

BRIGHTNESS & TEXT SIZE CHOICES

The Apple Watch's screen is quite tiny, so sometimes being able to adjust its look is useful, particularly when seeing the data in dim circumstances.

The Brightness & Text Size options include sliders that let you change the brightness of the screen, the size of text in all applications that support Dynamic Text, and a button that turns on and off a bold font that spans the whole screen.

SETTING SOUND & HAPTICS

Using the slider at the top of the screen, the Sound & Haptics settings regulate the loudness of all notifications. To control the strength of the taps you experience on your wrist during alerts, scroll down to the Haptic Strength slider.

Along with the aforementioned slider controls, the following buttons may also be found in this section:

When this option is turned on, audio alarms and notifications are silenced.

Prominent Haptic: When enabled, all standard notifications get an additional tap.

When you touch the Mickey or Minnie Mouse icon on the watch face, this setting—which is turned on by default—causes the watch to audibly proclaim the time.

PASSCODE SECURITY

The password on your watch is crucial because it prevents unauthorized people from accessing your private messages, data, and other sensitive information.

You may alter your existing four-digit code, activate or disable the Unlock with iPhone function, and disable or enable the passcode feature (not advised) under the Passcode settings area. As long as the watch is on your wrist and you unlock your phone using the Unlock with iPhone function, the watch will also unlock automatically.

CHAPTER FOUR
APPLE WATCH ICON MEANINGS

I t's likely that if you glance at the top of your Apple Watch's dial, at least one symbol, including the famed "red dot on Apple Watch," will be visible. While the Apple Watch shows a number of symbols on the dial, there are many more in locations like the Control Center. Here is your comprehensive reference on the meanings of every Apple Watch symbol in case you're still perplexed by them, like I was when I first began using the Apple Watch.

Note: WatchOS 9, the most recent Apple Watch operating system, has these icons.

ALL APPLE WATCH ICON MEANINGS (2022)

The definitions of each Apple Watch symbol seen in watchOS 8 have been covered in this chapter. To see a list of all the icon names, utilize the table of contents below.

STATUS ICON

1. RED DOT ICON

This indicator indicates that your Apple Watch has unread notifications. To see them, open the Notification Center by swiping down from the top. To access the Notification Center from inside an app, long press on the top edge of the screen and then slide down.

2. CHARGING ICON

Your Apple Watch's green flash indicator indicates that it is actively charging in its dock.

3. LOW BATTERY ICON

The Apple Watch battery is low if you see a red flash icon on your wrist. To recharge the battery, place your watch on the included charging cradle. If you often notice this indicator on your Apple Watch series 6, you should also read our article on how to extend its battery life.

4. LOCK ICON

When your Apple Watch has been secured with a password, the lock icon will show up. As soon as your watch is removed off your wrist, this occurs automatically. However, you may lock your Apple Watch via the Control Center if you've deactivated wrist detection.

You will need to input the passcode you created in order to open.

5. WATER LOCK ICON

Only Apple Watch Series 2 and later have this symbol. When the Water Lock mode is activated from the Control Center, it manifests. To avoid unintentional touches from being exposed to water, the Apple Watch does not react to touches in this mode.

To leave this mode on your watch, turn the Digital Crown until you hear a series of beeps. Additionally, this sound helps dry out the speakers on the Apple Watch.

6. DO NOT DISTURB ICON

When Do Not Disturb is on, the moon symbol appears. The presence of this indicator indicates that calls and warnings won't be audible or shown on the screen. Your alarms will still sound on the Apple Watch.

7. AIRPLANE MODE ICON

When Airplane Mode is activated on the Apple Watch, this symbol shows. The watch's wireless functionalities won't be accessible to you, but its non-wireless functionality will.

8. THEATER MODE ICON

This symbol denotes the presence of Theater Mode. This feature disables Always on Display and prevents the Apple Watch screen from lighting up when you get alerts.

The mode is designed to be used in movie theaters to prevent distractions, but I've discovered that it may be really useful if you wear your watch while sleeping.

9. WORKOUT ICON

When you are in the middle of an exercise, this symbol will show. To pause/end the exercise, touch on this symbol to be sent to the workout monitoring screen.

10. NO CELLULAR NETWORK ICON

If your Apple Watch (GPS + Cellular) has lost contact with the cellular network, this indicator will show up.

11. IPHONE DISCONNECTED ICON

If your Apple Watch and the iPhone it is linked with have been unpaired, this symbol will show up. If the issue persists, try bringing the devices closer together, disabling Airplane Mode, or restarting your watch.

12. IPHONE CONNECTED ICON

When your iPhone and Apple Watch are synced, this symbol shows in the Control Center.

13. LOCATION INDICATOR

When an app on your Watch has used or is utilizing your location, a location indicator appears. Be aware that if you are using a watch face that requires access to your location in order to display information like weather data, this signal will also appear.

14. WIFI ICON

When the Apple Watch is linked to a WiFi network, this symbol shows.

15. WIRELESS ACTIVITY ICON

When a wireless activity or active procedure is occurring, the Wireless Activity icon appears.

16. MIC ICON

A new orange mic symbol is included in watchOS 7. When your Watch is listening to audio, this appears. The microphone symbol will appear while you're speaking to Siri, recording a voice memo, or when the Apple Watch uses the microphone for additional functions like walkie-talkie and handwash detection.

17. LTE ICON

The LTE indicator will appear to indicate the strength of the signal if you're using a cellular Apple Watch.

18. NOW PLAYING ICON

When music is playing on your iPhone or Apple Watch, the Now Playing symbol appears. To control media playback and launch the Now Playing app, tap on this icon.

19. CALL ICON

This indicator appears while you're on a phone call, whether it's via your iPhone or the Apple Watch. To access the call screen, touch on this button.

20. MAPS ICON

When the Apple Maps app is being used to get directions, the Maps symbol appears on the Apple Watch.

21. NAVIGATION ICON

If a third-party mapping app is directing users on the Apple Watch, the navigation symbol appears on the watch.

22. WALKIE TALKIE ICON

When you activate Walkie Talkie mode on your watch, the walkie talkie symbol appears on the Apple Watch. The indicator indicates that you may be reached via walkie-talkie by your contacts.

23. CAR ICON

When the "Driving" focus mode is on on your iPhone, this symbol appears. Focus modes automatically sync across all of your Apple devices.

24. LOW POWER MODE ICON (YELLOW CIRCLE)

The Apple Watch Low Power Mode is activated if you see a yellow circle on the top of your watch face. You may disable this through the Control Center or by going to your watch's battery settings.

CONTROL CENTER AND APP ICONS

25. CELLULAR ICON

On Apple Watches with an eSIM, this symbol turns on or off the cellular connection.

26. WIFI ICON

On the Apple Watch, tapping on this symbol toggles WiFi.

27. PING IPHONE

Find your linked iPhone with the aid of this symbol. This causes your iPhone to beep loudly so you can find it when you tap on it.

Pro tip: To make it easier to locate in a dark setting, long-pressing this icon will cause your iPhone to flash its LED while playing the sound.

28. BATTERY PERCENTAGE

100%

This indicator displays your Apple Watch's current battery level. Additionally, pressing on this symbol displays a menu that includes a 'Power Reserve' option for your watch.

29. SILENT MODE

Toggle the Silent Mode on and off by tapping on this icon. To indicate which mode the Apple Watch is in, the symbol alternates between a standard bell and a crossed-out bell.

30. FLASHLIGHT

Your Apple Watch's flashlight should now be on. The watch has three different illumination modes. Swiping over the screen will allow you to choose one of them.

31. AIRPLAY ICON

You may choose the audio output you wish to utilize with your Apple Watch with this icon.

32. SLEEP MODE ICON

When it's time for bed, the Control Center and Apple Watch face display the sleep mode symbol (also known as the bed icon).

Your Apple Watch enters Do Not Disturb mode and disables the Always on Display when it is time to go to sleep. Your Apple Watch may be configured to monitor your sleep each night and wake you up with an alarm at a time of your choice.

33. SCHOOLTIME ICON

On the Apple Watch, the Control Center displays the Schooltime symbol. The watch's functionality are restricted during school hours when Schooltime is activated, and the symbol takes on a yellow hue.

If parents set up their child's Apple Watch using the Family Setup function on their iPhone, the feature is intended for children and may be scheduled by parents. The Control Center may also be used to toggle it.

34. PERSONAL FOCUS MODE ICON

When you activate "Personal" Focus Mode on your Apple Watch or any of your Apple devices, this symbol appears. It will appear in the control center and on the face of your Apple Watch.

35. WORK FOCUS MODE ICON

The Work icon appears when the "Work" focus mode is activated on your Apple Watch or any other Apple device, much like the Personal icon does. Both on the Apple Watch's face and in the control center, the emblem is visible.

GET TO KNOW YOUR APPLE WATCH BETTER

All of the icons and symbols that watchOS 9 on your Apple Watch may use are listed above. While many of these symbols are self-explanatory, some are a little bit more ambiguous than one may want.

CHAPTER FIVE
ADJUST BRIGHTNESS, TEXT SIZE, SOUNDS, AND HAPTICS

B oost the brightness. Tap the Brightness & Text Size option after opening the Settings app's Settings icon. To change the brightness, either touch the control and spin the digital crown. Alternatively, you may launch the Apple Watch app on your iPhone, choose My Watch, click Brightness & Text Size, and then move the Brightness slider.

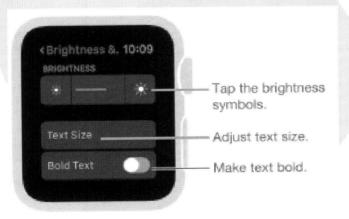

Increase text size. Open the Settings Settings button, then choose Brightness & Text Size by swiping down. Select Text Size, then select Letters or use the Digital Crown to scroll. Alternatively, you may launch the Apple Watch app on your iPhone, choose My Watch, select Brightness & Text Size, and then move the Text Size slider.

Bold text is used. Turn on Bold Text by selecting the Settings Settings icon, Brightness & Text Size, and scrolling down. Alternately, launch the Apple Watch app on your iPhone, choose My Watch, select Brightness & Text Size, and then enable Bold Text.

Apple Watch restarts to take effect of the update when you enable bold text on either the Apple Watch or iPhone.

Adapt the sound. Navigate to the Settings icon, choose Settings, and then select Sounds & Haptics. To change, press the slider or the volume controls under Alert Volume once, then spin the Digital Crown. Alternately, launch the Apple Watch app on your iPhone, choose My Watch, then select Sounds & Haptics before adjusting the Alert Volume slider.

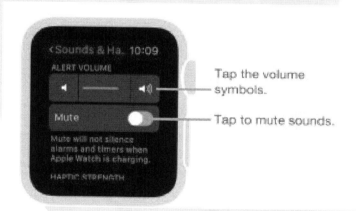

Apple Watch is muted. Turn on Mute after selecting Sounds & Haptics from the Settings Settings icon's scroll-down menu. Alternately, you may slide up on the watch display to get the Settings glance, then press the Silent Mode button. You may activate Silent Mode by opening the Apple Watch app on your iPhone, selecting My Watch, Sounds & Haptics, and then Silent Mode.

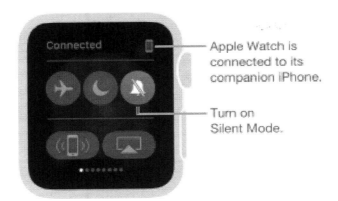

Apple Watch is connected to its companion iPhone.

Turn on Silent Mode.

By keeping your hand on the watch display for at least three seconds, you can fast silence alert and notification noises. In order to check that mute is on, you'll feel a tap. Make sure Cover to Mute is enabled in the Sounds & Haptics section of the Apple Watch app on your iPhone by tapping My Watch.

Change the haptic acuity. The wrist taps that Apple Watch utilizes for alerts and notifications may have their intensity changed. Navigate to the Settings icon, choose Settings, and then select Sounds & Haptics. Toggle it on by tapping the slider once or the haptic buttons under Haptic Strength, then crank the Digital Crown to adjust. Alternately, launch the Apple Watch app on your iPhone, choose My Watch, then select Sounds & Haptics before adjusting the Haptic Strength slider. For increased emphasis, activate prominent haptic.

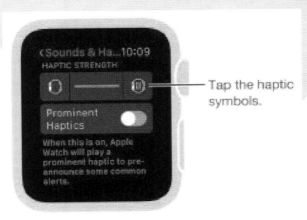

Tap the haptic symbols.

Turn on Do Not Disturb. Swipe up on the watch face, swipe left or right to the Settings look, then hit the Do Not Disturb button or symbol to prevent calls and notifications (except from alarms) from sounding or lighting up the screen. Alternately, hit the Do Not Disturb icon in the Settings menu to enable Do Not Disturb. The Do Not Disturb symbol will be seen at the top of the screen when Do Not Disturb is on.

Tap to turn on Do Not Disturb.

To silence both your Apple Watch and your iPhone, open the Apple Watch app on your iPhone, tap My Watch, then select General > Do Not Disturb > Mirror iPhone. Once you change Do Not Disturb on one, it will automatically change on the other to reflect the change.

TURN ON, WAKE, AND UNLOCK

Turn on your Apple Watch. In order to display the watch face if your Apple Watch is off, press and hold the side button until you see the Apple logo (there may first be a brief time of black screen).

Apple Watch OFFSET. Press and hold the side button until the sliders appear if you need to turn off your Apple Watch, and then slide the Power Off slider to the right. Typically, you'll wear your Apple Watch continuously.

Apple Watch is woken. Simply extend your wrist. When your wrist is lowered, Apple Watch goes back to sleep. Apple Watch may also be activated by pushing the Digital Crown or touching the screen.

Check your orientation settings again if your Apple Watch doesn't wake up when your wrist is raised. Open the Settings app, navigate to General > Orientation, and then press the Settings icon (if you're looking at the watch face) to confirm that Orientation is set to the wrist you wear Apple Watch on. In the Apple Watch app on your iPhone, you may also choose My Watch, General, and Watch Orientation to accomplish this. If Apple Watch doesn't wake up when you touch the screen or press the Digital Crown, it might need to be charged.

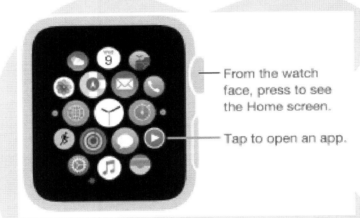

From the watch face, press to see the Home screen.

Tap to open an app.

Wake up to your watch face or the last thing you did. When Apple Watch wakes up, you may configure it to display the watch face or to take you back to the position you were in before it went to sleep. Open Settings Settings icon, choose General > Wake Screen, and switch on Wake Screen on Wrist Raise to make your selection. Then, choose your option under Resume To by scrolling down. You may also carry out this using the iPhone's Apple Watch app: Make sure Wrist Detection is set on, then touch General, My Watch, then Wake Screen.

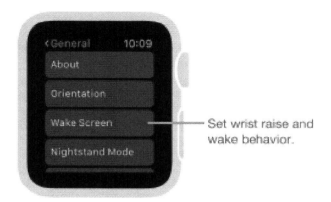

Set wrist raise and wake behavior.

Lock with an iPhone. Open the Apple Watch app on your iPhone, hit My Watch, tap Passcode, then enable Unlock with iPhone to unlock Apple Watch anytime you unlock your iPhone. Alternatively, on Apple Watch, hit the Settings icon, scroll down to Passcode, select it, and then toggle Unlock with iPhone on.

Note: You may use a separate passcode for your Apple Watch and iPhone; in fact, doing so is preferable.

Type in your passphrase. Apple Watch will request your password the next time you wake it up if you remove it from your wrist or wear it too loosely. Simply hit the number pad that displays with your passcode.

Modify your passphrase. Open the Settings Settings icon on your Apple Watch, scroll down to Passcode, press Change Passcode, and then follow the onscreen instructions. Alternately, you may launch the Apple Watch app on your iPhone, choose My Watch, Passcode, then Change Passcode, and then follow the onscreen instructions.

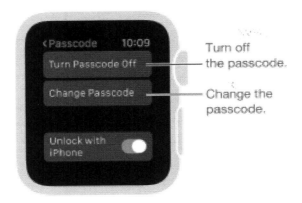

Turn off the passcode.

Change the passcode.

Make your passcode longer. To use a passcode longer than four numbers, open the Apple Watch app on your iPhone, select My Watch, Passcode, and then turn off Simple Passcode.

Disable the passcode. Open Settings, choose the Settings icon, select Passcode, and then select Turn Passcode Off. Alternately, open the Apple Watch app on your iPhone, choose My Watch, click Passcode, and then select Turn Passcode Off.

Note: You cannot use Apple Pay on Apple Watch if your passcode is disabled.

automatically lock. Activate wrist detection to have your watch lock itself while not being worn. Open the Apple Watch app on your iPhone, choose My Watch, General, and Wrist Detection, and then switch it on. You cannot use Apple Pay if Wrist Detection is disabled.

manually lock. Drag the Lock Device slider to the right after pressing and holding the side button to reveal the sliders. The next time you want to use Apple Watch, you must enter your passcode.

After ten unsuccessful unlock attempts, Apple Watch was wiped. In order to preserve the information on Apple Watch in the event that it is lost or stolen, you can set it up to destroy its data after 10 unsuccessful attempts to open it with the wrong passcode. Open the Apple Watch app on your iPhone, select My Watch, and then Passcode. Enable Erase Data lastly.

if you misplace your passphrase. To delete your Apple Watch settings and passcode, unpair it from your iPhone and then pair it again. Alternately, reset Apple Watch and link it with your iPhone once again.

USING HANDOFF

Thanks to several integrated features for its products and services, Apple undoubtedly has one of the greatest ecosystems available. If you want to make the most of the ecology, there is one of them things you must be aware of. Also known as Handoff.

With the help of the Handoff function, you may move between your Apple devices and pick up where you left off with your work. You should check this out if you are a member of the Apple ecosystem. Your Apple devices need to be signed in with the same Apple ID for Handoff to function.

So, what does this feature do and how might it simplify your life? This section explains how to utilize Handoff on all Apple devices and all of its capabilities.

Which Apple devices support Handoff?

A feature called handoff has existed for a lot longer than you would imagine. You don't trust me? Next, let's examine every Apple gadget that is Handoff-compatible.

iPhones, iPads, and iPods models that support Handoff

iPad: 4th generation or later

iPhones: iPhone 5 or later

iPad mini: All models

iPad Pro: All models

iPad Air: All models

iPad mini: All models

iPod touch: iPod touch 5th generation or later

Macs that support Handoff (OS X Yosemite or later)

MacBook 2015 and later later

MacBook Air 2012 and later later

MacBook Pro 2012 and later

Mac mini 2012 and later

iMac 2012 and later

Mac Pro 2013 and later

iMac Pro

Mac Studio

Besides, all Apple Watch models released since its inception have Handoff support.

HOW TO SET UP HANDOFF ON APPLE DEVICES

Let's examine how to set up the Handoff on Apple goods after establishing that your device is eligible for it. But before moving on, be sure that:

Conditions for using Handoff

Your Apple ID is used to log in to all of your Apple devices.

Wi-Fi is active on every device.

Make sure they are within 10 meters or 33 feet of one other and turn on Bluetooth.

In addition, you need to enable Handoff on each of your devices. But how can you pull it off? The procedures for each gadget are listed below.

ENABLE HANDOFF FOR MAC

System Settings may be accessed by clicking the Apple symbol.

Choose System Preferences for macOS Monetary or before.

Choose General.

Turn on Allow Handoff between this Mac and your iCloud devices at the bottom.

The same option should be enabled for macOS Monetary or earlier.

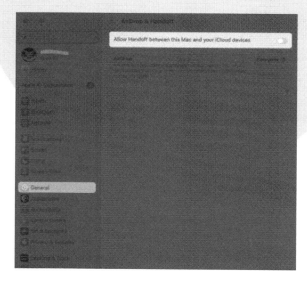

TURN ON HANDOFF FOR IPHONE, IPAD, AND IPOD TOUCH

Open Settings.

Tap General.

Select AirPlay & Handoff.

Toggle on Handoff.

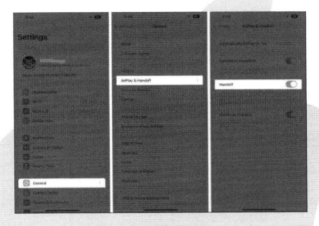

HOW TO TURN ON HANDOFF ON APPLE WATCH

Open the Watch app.

Tap General.

Scroll down and toggle on Enable Handoff.

USE HANDOFF ON APPLE DEVICES

It's time for us to utilize this function and simplify our life now that you have confirmed your device supports Handoff and followed the instructions to turn it on on your Apple devices. The applications that support Handoff are listed below.

Apps for iPhone, iPad, Mac, and Apple Watch that allow handoff:

Calendar

Reminders

Keynote

Safari, Pages

Mail

Contacts

Numbers

Maps

Note: In addition to them, numerous other third-party programs also support Handoff.

HOW TO UTILIZE THE HANDOFF FEATURE ON AN IPAD, IPHONE, AND MAC

It's considerably simpler than you may imagine to switch tasks from an iPhone to a Mac and vice versa. How to activate the functionality is as follows:

Open a Handoff-compatible app.

I am now opening Chrome on an iPhone..

After using the program for a while, shut it off.

Open the same program on your other device now.

I'm using a Mac here.

The prior device's icon will show up. Toggle the icon.

You can see the iPhone symbol above Chrome on a Mac in this picture.

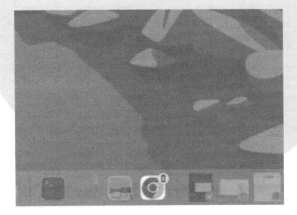

The browser Handoff symbol will be shown above the installed browser on Mac, regardless of whatever browser you use. If you are migrating from a Mac, the default browser on an iPhone or iPad is the same. The same holds true for other built-in programs.

Notably, you can now send the audio you hear on your iPhone to a HomePod in addition to sending the visual material from your Screen.

TURN AUTOMATIC AIRPLAY STREAMING ON/OFF

Users may transmit anything like images and movies using the AirPlay streaming function on Apple TV. The following is how to turn it on or off based on your preferences:

Open Settings and choose Airplay & Handoff

under General

Select AirPlay automatically to TVs.

You may choose one of the following alternatives from here:

Never: This will halt any streaming via AirPlay.

Your iPhone will prompt you to confirm your want to utilize the service.

Automatic: When this option is enabled, the iPhone and Apple TV will automatically connect.

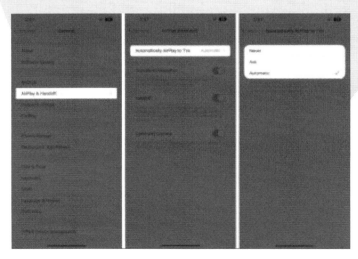

Note: Sharing clipboard items across your Apple devices is another fantastic aspect of the Apple ecosystem.

HOW TO TURN OFF HANDOFF ON IPHONE

If you are not interested in this function, you may easily turn it off while we are Handoff if it was not effective enough to get your hands in. Here is how to go about it:

For the iPod touch, iPhone, and iPad: Toggle off Handoff by opening Settings General AirPlay & Handoff.

Using a mac with Monterary or later: Toggle off Allow Handoff between this Mac and your iCloud devices in System Preferences / System Settings / General.

There it is.

I hope this section has helped you understand what Handoff is and how to use it on your Apple Watch, iPhone, iPad, Mac, and other devices. The handoff is an excellent tool. If you have any more queries or suggestions, don't hesitate to express them in the comments section.

CHAPTER SIX
USING APPLE WATCH WITHOUT ITS PAIRED IPHONE

One of the most comprehensive experiences available from the firm is the Apple Watch.

The electronic watch has grown to be one of the leading players in the wearable technology market since its debut in 2015. Apple has improved the Apple Watch with capabilities like GPS, LTE, and weatherproofing over the course of many iterations, but is it feasible to completely unpair it from the iPhone?

What an Apple Watch can really do without an iPhone's help is covered in this section.

CAN AN APPLE WATCH BE USED WITHOUT AN IPHONE?

Yes and no.

An iPhone is needed to set up an Apple Watch when you first receive one. There is no avoiding it. Without it, you basically have a lovely bracelet that is much too expensive and the iPhone Watch software handles most of the work.

We walk you through the steps for setting up an Apple Watch, but the truth of the matter is that you can't do it without an iPhone. Apple views the Apple Watch as an accessory for its smartphone, to the point that you can't even use an iPad or Mac to help set it up.

So why didn't we simply say "no," as opposed to "yes and no"? Although you can't set up an Apple Watch without an iPhone, you may use your iPhone to set up an Apple Watch for a kid or other family member who doesn't have an iPhone. Many of the Apple Watch's functionalities may still be used by them. For them to fully benefit, you must add them to your Family Sharing Group. However, they don't even need to be using cellular; instead, all they need is an Apple Watch that can connect to a Wi-Fi network in order to transmit or receive data. They will just need your iPhone's proximity to update the Apple Watch's software and make minor configuration changes.

Similar to this, even if you forgot your iPhone at home, you may still take use of several capabilities on your own Apple Watch. Below, we'll go through the uses for your Apple Watch that don't need an iPhone.

WHAT AN APPLE WATCH CAN DO WITHOUT AN IPHONE

All of the following functions may be performed by an Apple Watch without an iPhone in your pocket.

Your Apple Watch may sometimes need to be connected to a Wi-Fi or cellular network.

MONITOR EXERCISE AND ACTIVITY

Don't want to lug your iPhone on a run or a long stroll, but still want to shut your rings? While you're out and about, the Apple Watch will cheerfully track all of your steps and other health data. When you go home, if you have an iPhone, you can sync the data back up.

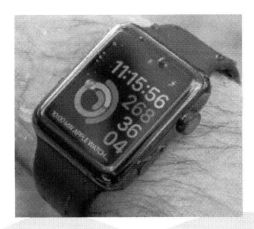

Employ additional health characteristics

Use the following Apple Watch functionalities even if you don't have an iPhone, Wi-Fi, or cellular service:

measure heart rate (all models)

Do an ECG (Apple Watch Series 4 or later.

Check your blood oxygen level (Apple Watch Series 6 or later)

Monitor sleep (Apple Watch Series 3 or later)

Medication monitoring (Apple Watch Series 4 or later)

Follow the menstrual cycle (Apple Watch Series 1 or later)

LISTEN TO MUSIC

You can store a lot of songs on the Apple Watch itself, all of which can be listened to without the need for an iPhone, whether you want to listen to some upbeat music while working out or simply enjoy listening to a podcast or album as you putter about in the yard. A set of Bluetooth headphones are obviously necessary as an Apple Watch lacks a headphone port unless you want the small speakers to spoil your workout and your relationship with the neighbors.

If you have a cellular connection or are linked to Wi-Fi, you can also stream music via Apple Music.

LISTEN TO PODCASTS AND AUDIOBOOKS

You can listen to podcasts and audiobooks that you've synchronized with your Apple Watch even when there isn't a Wi-Fi or cellular connection. Additionally, you may stream them if you can connect to a Wi-Fi or cellular network.

READ NEWS

You will need a Wi-Fi or cellular connection for this one as well, but even if your iPhone is not nearby, you can still check the most recent news on the News app and keep track of stocks.

CALL PEOPLE AND GET CALLS

You can configure your Apple Watch to function as an extension of your iPhone if it has cellular capabilities and is a Series 3 model or later and is linked to a Wi-Fi network. Then, even if your iPhone is at home hidden in a drawer, you'll be able to make and receive calls immediately on your Watch.

While there are extra fees associated with utilizing the eSIM capability, you'll find them to be far less onerous than the regular carrier plans.

SEND AND RECEIVE TEXT MESSAGES

Similar to phone calls, you may send and receive messages on your Apple Watch as long as you are connected to Wi-Fi or cellular data.

SENDING AND READING EMAILS

The same is true for emails; you may access them without an iPhone as long as you are connected to Wi-Fi or a cellular network.

APPLY MAPS

The Apple Watch's ability to utilize the Apple Maps app without an iPhone nearby is another really helpful feature. Once again, a cellular plan or a Wi-Fi connection are required for this. You may now move about freely without carrying an expensive, bulky iPhone in your pocket.

Without a network connection, you may use the compass to determine which direction is north.

USE APPLE PAY

You may not be aware of this, but after you've set up Apple Pay on your Apple Watch, you can pay for items at the register without needing to have your iPhone with you. Simply double-press the Side button and place the Watch over the contactless sensor to complete the transaction.

CAN AN ANDROID PHONE BE USED WITH AN APPLE WATCH?

No. You may infer that Android phones are further down the list if Apple doesn't want the Watch to function with iPads and Macs.

It's plausible that Apple views the Watch as a system-seller since users may choose to keep using their iPhones in order to utilize the Apple Watch. The corporation is not under any big pressure to start supporting additional platforms for the devices any time soon.

CHAPTER SEVEN

HOW TO USE BLUETOOTH HEADPHONES WITH AN APPLE WATCH

Wired headphones are not an option since the Apple Watch lacks a headphone connector (or a Lighting port, for that matter). But the watch is compatible with any set of Bluetooth headphones.

PAIR YOUR HEADPHONES

To begin, you must first link your headphones with your watch; how you accomplish this will depend on the specific headphones you are using.

Start the headphones' pairing process. On most of these gadgets, a button must be pressed and held down for a certain amount of time—typically until a light begins blinking. However, you should review the headphones' accompanying instructions.

Turn to the Apple Watch and launch the Settings app after they are in pairing mode. (To access the applications page, press the Digital Crown. Then, hit the cogs symbol.) On the main Settings screen, choose Bluetooth, which is the third option from the top.

The top portion of the watch will advise you that it is looking for devices, and the bottom section will identify health devices. Any devices that are found will be mentioned in those sections, along with information about whether or not they are linked to the watch. When your headphones appear, tap them.

Depending on the security settings and features of your headphones, you could now be required to enter a PIN or password.

There can be a little delay while the matching procedure is finished.

HOW TO DOWNLOAD MUSIC TO APPLE WATCH

If you know where to search, downloading music to your Apple Watch is a rather straightforward procedure. Here's how to add music to your Apple Watch and download it.

Tap the Apple Watch app on your attached iPhone.

Tap Music as you go down. (You may have to first choose your Apple Watch from a list.)

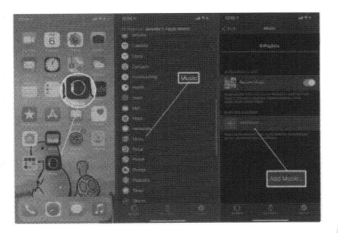

Find the song that you want to add by searching through your music library.

Select Add Music.

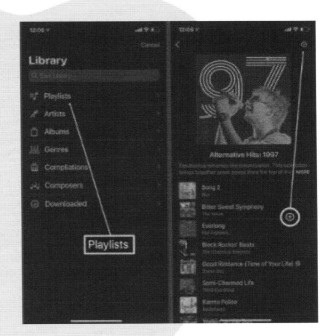

Select the album or playlist you wish to add to your Apple Watch by tapping the + sign next to it.

Can Apple Watch Play Music Offline?

Yes, provided that your Apple Watch has adequate capacity. Here's how to go about it.

Tap the Music app on your Apple Watch.

Press Library.

To discover the content you wish to download, tap Playlists, Artists, or Albums.

Simply tap the desired song or album.

Click on the three dots.

Select Download.

Your Apple Watch will now download the music so you may listen to it offline.

HOW CAN I DOWNLOAD MUSIC TO MY APPLE WATCH WITHOUT USING MY IPHONE?

If you subscribe to Apple Songs, you may instantly add music using your Apple Watch. Here's how to go about it.

Tap the Music app on your Apple Watch.

To locate the album or playlist you wish to add, tap Library, Listen Now, or Search.

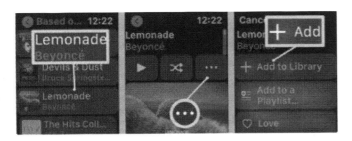

Click the album.

Click on the three dots.

Click Add to Library.

You may now stream the music on your Apple Watch. Follow the instructions above to download it for offline listening.

CAN I DOWNLOAD SONGS FROM SPOTIFY TO MY APPLE WATCH?

Songs from Spotify may be downloaded to your Apple Watch for offline or online listening. You must have a Spotify Premium account in order to listen to music offline. This is how you can download music.

Tap Spotify on your Apple Watch.

swipe left to access Your Library.

Select Your Library.

You may download a playlist or album by tapping it.

Click on the three dots.

On the Apple Watch, choose Download. Now the album or song will download.

HOW TO CREATE A PLAYLIST FOR EXERCISE ON YOUR APPLE WATCH

Using the Workout app, you may create a playlist that will start playing whenever you begin working out. Here is what to do.

Choose the Apple Watch app on your iPhone.

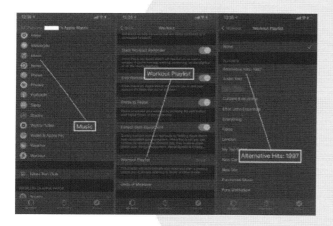

Tap Exercise.

Toggle to Workout Playlist. To find this, you may need to scroll down.

Select the playlist you want to start playing every time you start working out by tapping it.

HOW DO I ERASE MUSIC FROM MY APPLE WATCH?

Tap My Watch, then scroll down and tap Music in the Watch app on your iPhone. If you wish to delete any music from your Apple Watch, hit Edit, then press Delete.

CHAPTER EIGHT
HOW TO USE THE FOCUS FEATURE

You'll undoubtedly agree that the Apple Watch offers unparalleled functionality, yet it may also serve as a distraction in many situations. With the release of Focus, a function that is similar to DND but has additional options and customization, Apple provided a remedy for this. Learn how to configure Focus on your Apple Watch so that you may concentrate more on your life.

HOW TO INITIATE AN APPLE WATCH FOCUS (CUSTOM FOCUS)

Your Apple Watch may have a personalized Focus. You must do this on your iPhone, however. Your Apple Watch will display the customized Focus you've designed. How to do it is as follows:

Access the iPhone settings.

Select Focus.

In the upper right corner, click the Plus symbol.

To make a unique Focus, tap Custom.

Now, finish the setup by following the on-screen directions.

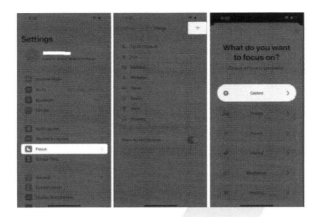

HOW TO TURN ON FOCUS ON APPLE WATCH

To open Control Center, swipe upward from the bottom of the screen.

Hold the crescent moon emblem in your hand.

choosing a focus mode.

Focus may be activated by selecting On, On for 1 hour, or On till tomorrow morning.

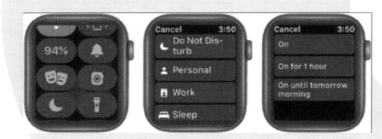

TURN OFF FOCUS ON APPLE WATCH

If a Focus is activated, your Apple Watch Face will show its icon. To disable it,

Start the Control Center app on your Apple Watch.

Select Focus mode by tapping it.

To disable Focus mode, press the icon for it while it's activated.

CREATE A FOCUS SCHEDULE ON APPLE WATCH

Many of us have everyday routines. On weekdays, if you work from 9 am to 5 pm and go to the gym every morning from 6 to 7, you may set up several Focus modes to automatically activate at the appropriate times. This is how:

Launch Settings.

Select Focus.

Decide on a Focus.

Here, I'll use the example of Work.

Click the "Add new..." link.

Set the on and off times accordingly.

Choose the days you want it to turn on under Repeat.

HOW TO DELETE OR DISABLE A FOCUS SCHEDULE ON APPLE WATCH

Go to Settings and choose Focus.

Choose the Focus you wish to remove or turn off.

Tap the schedule you wish to remove or deactivate on the next screen.

Scroll down and switch off the Focus now.

By pressing the Delete button, you may also remove the Focus.

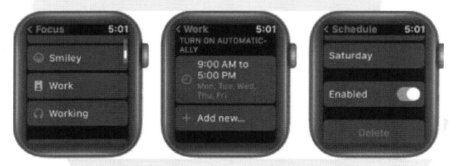

Connect a Focus to all of your devices.

Go to Settings and choose Focus.

Click on Mirror my iPhone in the lower right corner.

Focus will now turn on on your iPhone when you turn it on on your Apple Watch going forward!

WHAT IS FOCUS MODE?

Focus is comparable to the Do Not Disturb setting, but it has a wider range of features than the default setting.

WHICH IS PREFERABLE, FOCUS OR DO NOT DISTURB?

The ability to arrange focus depending on time, place, etc. makes it easier. Additionally, you may choose various permissions for various Focus modes.

DOES THE FOCUS MODE PREVENT CALLS?

Not all calls are blocked by focus mode. No matter whether Focus mode you are in, calls from emergency contacts are always enabled. You may decide whether or not to permit calls from other contacts, however.

HOW DO I CHANGE MY WATCH FACE ON FOCUS?

Select Create Personal Automation or Add from the Automation tab in Shortcuts after opening it. Choose a mode under Create Personal Automation, then touch When Turning On, Next, Add Action. select or lookup Create Watch Face Choose the choice under "Set active watch face to" at the bottom. Select the Apple Watch face, then select Next. disabling Ask Before Running Verify Don't Ask now and hit Done.

CHAPTER NINE
HOW TO MEASURE BLOOD OXYGEN LEVEL

The pulse oximeter included in the Apple Watch Series 6, 7, 8, and Watch Ultra enables them to non-invasively gauge your general health by calculating the proportion of oxygen delivered by red blood cells from the lungs to the rest of your body.

The term "blood oxygen levels" (also known as "SpO2") refers to the average blood oxygen levels of most individuals, but not all, which typically range from 95% to 100%.

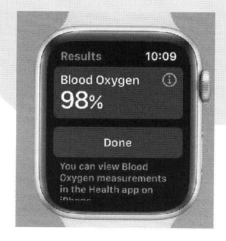

WHAT IS BLOOD OXYGEN MONITORING?

Blood oxygen levels, also known as SpO2, are the percentage of oxygen carried by red blood cells from the lungs to the rest of the body as well as how successfully this oxygenated blood is being transported.

The Apple Watch Series 6 and Series 7 and other wearables employ pulse oximetry, which is basically a simplified way of expressing "non-invasive oxygen saturation monitoring," to be able to alert the user when their blood oxygen level drops below a specific level.

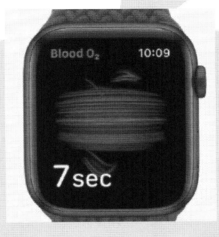

Anything that is over 95% is often regarded as "normal." Anything less than 92%, however, may be a sign of a health problem, such as sleep apnea.

For instance, Fitbit explicitly tracks changes and variability in blood oxygen levels throughout recorded sleep periods using the SpO2 sensor in its wearables. Similar to its ECG monitoring feature, the Apple Watch examines the user's SpO2 levels while they are motionless, and readings only take 15 seconds. Additionally, periodic measurements will be made silently while you sleep and are not moving.

What other benefits can blood oxygen monitoring provide? According to John Hopkins Medicine, pulse oximetry can be used to determine whether a person requires assistance with their breathing (via a ventilator), determine their capacity for strenuous physical activity, and, as we previously mentioned, determine whether breathing temporarily stops while they are sleeping (sleep apnea).

HOW DOES BLOOD OXYGEN MONITORING WORK?

How does the test, which was previously only available on specialized monitors, function on smartwatches and fitness trackers?

Well, historically, SpO2 monitors were attached to the user's finger or toe via a clip-on device. Then, it would employ red and infrared light sensors to record, for instance, the amount of oxygen moving through the finger and continually check for changes.

Of course, in the contemporary sense, this may now be done straight from the wrist without any modifications. In order to measure the light reflected back from the blood, Apple clearly states that it employs four clusters of green, red, infrared, and LEDs and four photodiodes on the rear crystal of the Series 6.

HOW TO USE THE APPLE WATCH TO MEASURE BLOOD OXYGEN LEVELS

You must have an iPhone 6S or later, the Apple Watch Series 6, 7, 8, or Watch Ultra, be above the age of 18, be in a country that is compatible (see the bottom of this feature), and meet the other requirements.

Additionally, you should check to see whether the Blood Oxygen app is configured; if not, see the section below this feature.

If all the preceding conditions are met, conduct a blood oxygen measurement by following these steps:

- A tight fit for your Apple Watch should be achieved.
- Open the app list or view by pressing the Digital Crown.
- Activate the Blood Oxygen app (red and blue circle)

- Make sure you remain motionless, the Apple Watch face is up, and place your arm on a table or in your lap.
- Hit "Start"
- Do not move for 15 seconds.
- After 15 seconds, your findings will be shown on the screen.

Tap Done!

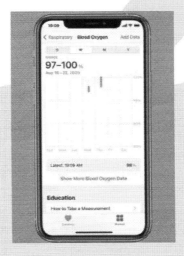

Where to get your Apple Watch blood oxygen readings

Both on-demand and background blood oxygen readings made by the Apple Watch Series 6, Series 7, Series 8, and Watch Ultra are shown in the iPhone's Health app.

The steps listed below should help you determine your blood oxygen levels:

On an iPhone, launch the Health app.

Click the Browse button.

Select Respiratory.

Blood oxygenation

Select "Show More Blood Oxygen" Info to learn more

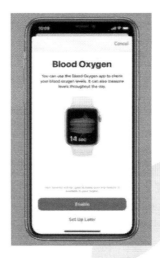

HOW TO INSTALL BLOOD OXYGEN ON APPLE WATCH

These instructions will assist you in setting up your Apple Watch's blood oxygen sensor if you haven't done so before. Following the setup procedures listed below, the Blood Oxygen app is installed. You may retrieve it through the Apple Watch App Store if you unintentionally erase it.

- Get your iPhone's Health app open.
- Hit the Browse button.
- Respiratory Tap
- Toggle Blood Oxygen
- To set up blood oxygen, click.
- Observe the guidelines

WHERE CAN I GET THE BLOOD OXYGEN APP?

There are just a few nations and locations where the Blood Oxygen app is accessible.

CHAPTER TEN
VIEWING AND RESPONDING TO YOUR MESSAGES

The ability to read text messages and other alerts from your iPhone by merely raising your wrist when you feel a little touch is one of the most practical features of an Apple Watch.

After reading a message, you can send a brief reply from your Apple Watch, but for anything lengthier, you should definitely pull out your iPhone and send a text the old-fashioned manner.

Here's how it's done.

How to use your Apple Watch to read SMS messages

1. As soon as the message arrives, raise your wrist.

2. To check your notifications if you don't notice the message right away, swipe down on the Watch face. The list of unread messages may be seen here.

3. Press the Digital Crown to see all of your applications, then touch the Messages icon to see a message you've previously opened (bright green with a white chat bubble).

4. The Dock may also be used to access Messages. Press the side button, then navigate through your most recently used applications with your finger or the Digital Crown.

5. If Do Not Disturb is on, you must check your iPhone for text message alerts since all incoming texts will be muffled.

HOW DO YOU RESPOND TO TEXT MESSAGES, ON YOUR APPLE WATCH?

When you reach the last post or thread, there are numerous methods to reply.

Text message dictation

By pressing the microphone icon, speaking into it, and adding any necessary punctuation, you may dictate a text reply. When you're done, click Send..

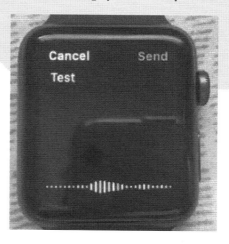

Open the Watch application on your iPhone if you'd rather send audio messages with this feature or want both choices accessible. Tap Messages, then Dictated Messages, and then choose Transcript (the default), Audio, or Transcript or Audio under the My Watch menu.

WITH SCRIBBLE, SEND A PERSONALIZED RESPONSE

Using Scribble, a function that allows you to scribble on an Apple Watch face, you may also send a personalized response.

First, touch the symbol while directing the finger toward a row of dots.

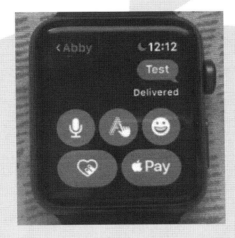

The watch will then convert the letters, words, numbers, and punctuation you write with your finger into text.

The Digital Crown may be used to change a letter, or you can choose predictive text to finish your sentence. Once you've completed crafting your message, tap Send.

SEND AN EMOJI

By pressing the happy face symbol, you may send an emoji.

Then, just touch on the emoji you want to send. Emojis that you use the most often will be shown at the top of the menu.

SEND A PRESET REPLY

Scroll through the circular icons for other sorts of answers to use a pre-set response (such as "OK" or "On my way"). To send the appropriate response, tap it.

On the iPhone Watch app, you can even design your own pre-reply. Select the My Watch tab, then select Messages, followed by Default Replies. If you want to alter a default reply, just touch on it. If you want to delete a default reply or modify the order in which it appears in the scroll, simply hit Edit.

REACT BY TAPPING BACK

Finally, by double pressing the relevant text message and choosing your answer, you may tapback (reply in-line to a specific text message) (a heart, a thumbs up, a thumbs down, etc.).

ON THE APPLE WATCH, HOW TO SEND A NEW SMS MESSAGE

Launch the Messages application.

2. Press New Message by pressing firmly on the display until you feel a light tap.

3. Select a recent contact from the list that displays when you press Add Contact, click Contacts to browse additional contacts, or click Keypad to input a phone number.

4. Any of the aforementioned techniques may be used to compose your message; after completed, hit Send.

CHAPTER ELEVEN
HOW TO USE APPLE WATCH TO MAKE AND ANSWER CALLS

Have you ever imagined a day when we could make calls directly from our wrists? Even though it still appears like something out of science fiction, Apple Watch allows you to place and receive phone calls. Apple Watch routes calls via the iPhone, but you can respond even if your phone is in another room or in your pocket and carry on a full conversation from your watch by doing so.

Taking a Call

It should go without saying to answer a phone call. Simply hit the green answer button when the call is received. You may choose to send the call to voicemail if you don't want to answer it by tapping the red refuse button.

You have the option of sending a text message or answering the call on your iPhone. To access these choices when the call is received, turn the Digital Crown or swipe upward.

If you are in a meeting or otherwise distracted and forget to switch off your Apple Watch, you may instantly silence the sound of an incoming call by covering the display with your palm for three seconds. After that, tap one more to confirm that mute is turned on.

TO ACTIVATE THE COVER TO MUTE FUNCTION:

- On your iPhone, launch the Apple Watch app.
- From the menu, choose Sounds and Haptics.
- Turn on Cover to Mute by flipping the switch.

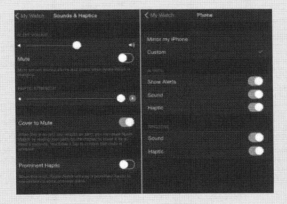

TURNING OFF SOUND OR HAPTIC ALERTS:

On the Apple Watch, you can turn the sound or the haptic ringtones and alerts on and off, but you can't customize specific ringtones as you can on the iPhone. The Apple Watch is configured to mirror the iPhone by default, but you may customize the alert and ringtone settings on the iPhone by using the Apple Watch app.

- On your iPhone, launch the Apple Watch app.
- Find "Phone" in the app area by scrolling down.
- Use the Ringtone toggles to turn off sound or haptic alerts for incoming calls.

- Select which notifications to receive by tapping "Custom" after which you may customize alerts (for missed and incoming calls).

You will get a notice on your Apple Watch if you quiet a call and the caller leaves you a voicemail. To listen to a voicemail, either open the Phone app on your Apple Watch and choose Voicemail, or press the voicemail notice.

Use the Handoff function on the iPhone's lock screen to switch to your iPhone after answering the call on your Apple Watch (swipe up from the phone icon in the bottom left corner). If your iPhone is still locked, tap the green bar at the top of the screen to unlock it.

MAKING A CALL

By pressing the Side button just below the Digital Crown, you may call individuals on your Favorites list. Next, choose by turning the Digital Crown or tapping a person's initials. In the lower left corner of the screen, touch the call symbol after that.

To call someone who isn't on your Favorites list, open the Phone app on your Apple Watch and swipe or spin the Digital Crown to the person's name. By saying "Call" and selecting a person from your contact list, you may also ask Siri to place a call on your behalf. You may make the call using Siri.

Talking on Apple Watch first seems a little unusual, and you may want to avoid doing it in public for the simple reason that background noise might make it difficult to hear someone via the Apple Watch speaker. But if you need to speak to someone and your iPhone is not handy, using the Apple Watch to make a call is tremendously useful. Additionally, you may take your time going to your iPhone, answer the call on Apple Watch, and then switch back when you're ready. No more unanswered calls.

CHAPTER TWELVE
HOW TO USE COMPASS WAYPOINTS ON AN APPLE WATCH

The revised Compass app may be used to construct Compass Waypoints and then determine the distance and direction between them on the Apple Watch SE, Apple Watch Ultra, and Apple Watch Series 6 and later. This is how it goes.

The Compass app has been updated in watchOS 9 and now has an adaptable watch face that displays your bearing in the middle. You may see your inclination, elevation, and coordinates in the inner ring of the compass by scrolling the Digital Crown.

The Compass ring will display the position of any Waypoints you construct. You may mark and display Compass Waypoints using the procedures below.

HOW TO DISPLAY AND MARK WAYPOINTS

To add a waypoint, press the waypoint symbol in the bottom-left portion of the Compass app's screen.

Choose the waypoint's title, color, and symbol (home, for instance) as you choose, and then touch Done.

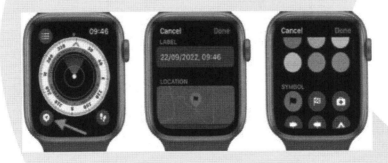

Hit a waypoint on any of the three Compass displays, use the Digital Crown to choose a waypoint from the list, then tap Select to see the waypoint. (Note the waypoint's location and direction, such as "Arrived" or "2.5 miles to your right.")

The waypoint will appear on a map with its coordinates when you tap the pen symbol towards the bottom of the screen.

By pressing the three-lines symbol in the top-left corner of any Compass screen, you may access all of the waypoints you've made. You may discover the co-ordinates stated below the coordinates, along with a choice to add a bearing, by simply scrolling down.

Delete Waypoints:

- On any Compass screen, click the three lines in the top-left corner.
- Swipe left across the waypoint you wish to eliminate as you scroll down to the list of them.
- The red X that appears should be tapped.

A Delete Waypoint button may be found by tapping a waypoint and scrolling to the bottom of its screen. Instead of removing a waypoint, you might choose to conceal it instead: Simply turn the Show Waypoint switch off.

CREATE A COMPASS WAYPOINT ON THE WATCH FACE.

You may rapidly travel to waypoints you've set, the last waypoint you saw in the Compass app, or your parked vehicle using the Compass Waypoint complication on your Apple Watch face.

- Choose a watch face with complications, then touch and hold the display while it is visible, then hit Edit.

- Tap one of the complication slots after highlighting them with a left swipe all the way to the end.

- To add a waypoint as a complication, either scroll to "Compass Waypoints," select one of the first three listed waypoints, or press More, then tap a waypoint, Last Viewed Waypoint, or Parked Car Waypoint.

- Tap the face to switch to it after pressing the Digital Crown to save your changes.

Once the complication has been added, you may press it to have the waypoint shown in the Compass app.

CHAPTER THIRTEEN
HOW TO CHARGE AN APPLE WATCH

Configure the charger. Put the supplied Apple Watch Magnetic Charging Cable or Apple Watch Magnetic Charging Case on a level surface in a well-ventilated location, connect it to the included power adapter, and then connect the adapter to an electrical outlet.

Sync up your Apple Watch. Place the Apple Watch's back on the charger. Apple Watch is correctly aligned by magnets on the charger. Keep the Apple Watch Magnetic Charging Case opened when using it. If Apple Watch is not muted, a bell will sound when charging starts, and a charging icon will appear on the watch face. While Apple Watch needs a charge, the sign is red; when it is receiving one, it is green.

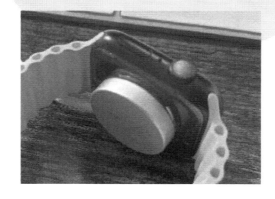

Verify the remaining power. Swipe up on the watch face of your Apple Watch, then choose the Battery look.

Numerous watch faces, including Modular, Color, Utility, Simple, Chronograph, and Mickey Mouse, allow you to add the battery indication. Firmly press the display while the watch face is visible, choose Customize, and then slide to the left until you can select certain feature positions. After selecting Battery using the Digital Crown, tap a place and push it to leave.

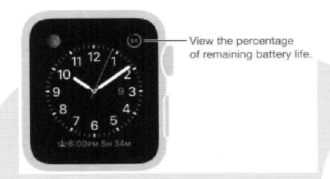

View the percentage of remaining battery life.

To extend the power at your disposal, use Power Reserve. When the battery is running low, you may place Apple Watch in Power Reserve mode to save energy. The time is still shown on Apple Watch, however other applications cannot be used. Tap Power Reserve after moving your finger up to the Battery glimpse on the watch display. The Power Reserve slider may also be accessed by pressing the side button and dragging it to the right.

Apple Watch warns you and provides you the option to activate Power Reserve mode when the battery level decreases to 10%.

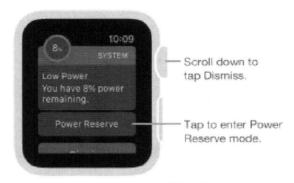

Apple Watch automatically switches into Power Reserve mode when its battery is almost empty.

revert to the default power mode. Press and hold the side button to restart your Apple Watch until you see the Apple logo. Apple Watch cannot resume unless the battery has at least a 10% charge.

Check the amount of time since the last charge. Go to General > Usage after opening the Apple Watch app on your iPhone and selecting My Watch.

CHAPTER FOURTEEN
HOW TO USE THE APP STORE ON YOUR APPLE WATCH

Over time, the Apple Watch has undergone tremendous change. You can perform a lot of things right now on your Apple Watch without ever picking up your iPhone.

The App Store is a fantastic illustration. With only a few clicks, you can access the App Store on your Apple Watch. True, the App Store on your iPhone has a lot more functionality and is still simpler to use.

However, stay reading to learn more about what the Apple Watch App Store can achieve.

1. CHECK YOUR PURCHASED APPS

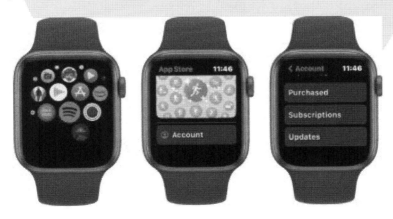

The App Store adds the app you purchase and download to your list of purchases. Then, if you wish to redownload any purchased applications, you may visit that list to locate them all. The best feature is that you don't need an iPhone to see this list. All you have to do is acquire an Apple Watch and do the following actions:

- Toggle the Digital Crown.
- On your home screen, click the App Store icon
- Tap Account towards the bottom of the page as you scroll down.
- Click Purchased.
- Choose My Purchases

The end. A list of all the applications you've bought will be shown. On the right side of the app, there will be an icon to download it once more to your Apple Watch or a button to open it if it has already been loaded. You can also click it to learn more about the app.

Remember that if the app is available, installing it on your Apple Watch will also install it on your iPhone.

2. MANAGE YOUR SUBSCRIPTIONS

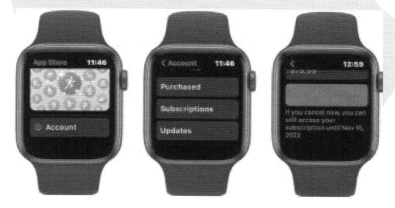

You can manage your subscriptions using nothing more than your Apple Watch, which may seem absurd to some. Although checking and canceling your membership on an iPhone or iPad still makes it simpler, it's a good idea to know how to do it on an Apple Watch as well.

- For access to your Home Screen, press the Digital Crown.
- Select App Store.
- At the bottom of the page, pick Account.
- Choose subscriptions.

A list of all your current subscriptions will be shown. You just need to press the subscription, scroll to the bottom, choose Cancel Membership, and then confirm that you wish to cancel your subscription if you want to do so.

In the event that additional subscription options become available, you may also change your plan using your Apple Watch.

3. INSTALLING APPS DIRECTLY ON YOUR APPLE WATCH

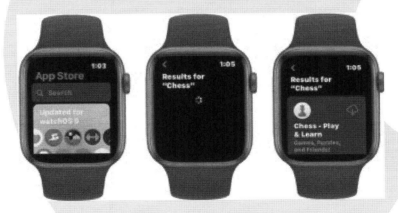

Every app you download for your iPhone may now now be loaded on your Apple Watch by changing the settings in the Watch app on your iPhone (whenever an Apple Watch app is available).

However, you may utilize the Apple Watch's Software Store to search and download any available app if you wish to install it directly on your device.

To access your Home Screen on your Apple Watch, press the Digital Crown.

- Activate the App Store.

- Click Search.

- Find the software you want to install by searching.

- From the search results, choose the desired app.

- Click Get.

The app will be installed on your Apple Watch and added to your Home Screen. After there, you may start using the app and, if you'd like, add it to your Apple Watch Dock.

If you're a new Apple Watch user, there are many fantastic applications available for download. Browse around to discover the best apps and games for you.

4. UTILIZE THE APP STORE'S SUGGESTIONS TO YOUR ADVANTAGE

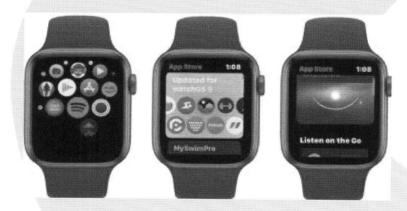

For new users, making the most of the Apple Watch could be difficult. You only need to download the countless amazing programs that are readily available for new Apple Watch users to improve your life.

But where do you even begin? The Apple Watch's App Store, however, suggests a number of excellent applications for you to utilize.

There is something for everyone, from Apple Watch Starter Kits to applications updated for the most recent watchOS software upgrade. You just need to scroll down after the App Store has opened on your Apple Watch—as we previously demonstrated—to see all of Apple's top recommendations.

5. LEARN EVERYTHING ABOUT AN APP BEFORE DOWNLOADING IT

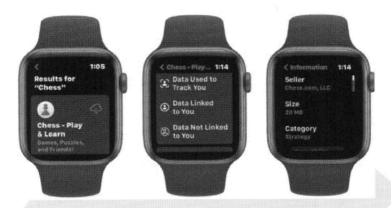

Your iPhone's App Store does an excellent job of informing you of all the data an app needs before you download it. And thankfully, the Apple Watch also provides you with quick access to all of that information. As follows:

- For access to your Home Screen, press the Digital Crown.
- Activate the App Store.
- Look for the desired app.
- To access additional information, tap the app.
- To see more details on the app, scroll down below the ratings.

You may discover a lot of information here, including a list of all the ratings and reviews that other users have left as well as the data that the program needs to manage in order to function effectively.

Additionally, you may go to the bottom and choose Information if you want to learn additional details about the app. If you want to buy an Apple Watch for your children, you will discover all the information you require about the app, including who is selling it, the languages it supports, and the app's age rating.

6. MANUALLY UPDATE YOUR APPS

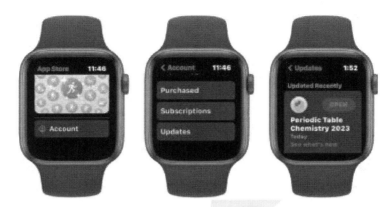

The Apple Watch will automatically update your apps on a regular basis by default. Get a list of the applications that need updating and update them yourself if you don't want to wait for your Watch to complete the task. Following these steps:

- When you tap the Digital Crown, the Home Screen will show up.
- Tap the symbol for the App Store.
- At the bottom of the page, click Account.
- Scroll down one more, then click Updates.

Here, you can get a list of all the apps that can receive updates as well as all the apps that have recently gotten updates. To check whether an app has received an update, tap Update next to its name. If you have a lot of open programs, you may want to choose Update All.

LEARN TO USE THE APPLE WATCH APP STORE

It goes without saying that using the App Store on an iPhone or iPad is quicker and simpler. Having saying that, understanding how to access the App Store on your Apple Watch might sometimes be useful. There are a ton more things you may attempt to get the most out of your Apple Watch; this is just the tip of the iceberg.

CHAPTER FIFTEEEN
APPLE WATCH WON'T UPDATE?

The Apple Watch is a stunning and powerful gadget. Its software has to be updated often for maintenance and bug fixes, much like your iPhone. What happens, however, if the Apple Watch upgrade won't run? You might find the following troubleshooting advice useful if your Apple Watch won't update.

How Come My Apple Watch Won't Update? Steps for Troubleshooting

There are several reasons why an Apple Watch update might not install. Try this first if the update is still not beginning after your iPhone is up to date and your Apple Watch is charged. If you've previously done this, I'll go through the steps to correct the "Unable to Install Update" problem on an Apple Watch and the prerequisites for the most recent software update to make sure your watch is compatible.

- Before trying the update again, restart your iPhone and Apple Watch.
- If the problem continues, unpair your Apple Watch from your iPhone.
- Link your iPhone and Apple Watch.

Continue reading or click the links for step-by-step directions on how to resolve your Apple Watch not updating difficulties to discover the precise procedures for each of them.

1. Restart Your Apple Watch

On an Apple Watch, there is no restart option as there is on an iPhone; you must turn the watch off and then on again. How to restart your Apple Watch is as follows:

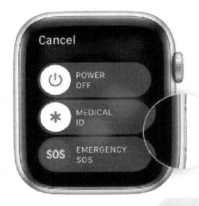

Try and hold down the Side button.

There will be many sliders.

Power Off slider: move to the right.

The Watch will power off after 30 seconds, so wait until the Apple Logo displays before clicking the side button to turn it back on.

2. Decouple your iPhone's Apple Watch from it.

After completing the above instructions, unpair the Apple Watch if it still won't update. If the Apple Watch won't update, use these steps to unpair it from your iPhone:

Getting your iPhone's Watch app

While on the My Watch page, tap the All Watches button at the top of the screen.

Next to the watch you want to unpair, tap the info symbol.

Select Unpair Apple Watch.

Tap Unpair [Name's] Apple Watch to unpair.

3. After unpairing your Apple Watch from your iPhone, here is how to re-pairing your Apple Watch from your iPhone:

Aside from turning it on by tapping the side button until the Apple logo shows, be sure your Apple Watch is turned on.

Open the Watch app on your iPhone.

Tap Start Pairing.

You may then decide whether to set it up for a relative or for yourself.

Place your Apple Watch within the phone's yellow frame. Alternately, you have the option to pair manually.

After your device has been connected, you can either tap Set Up as New Apple Watch to start anew or touch Recover from Backup to restore it from a previous Watch backup.

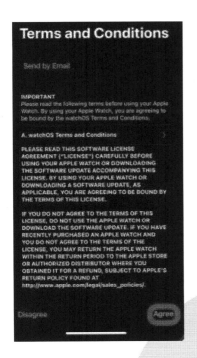

You'll see more options with instructions. Continue to follow the on-screen instructions to complete the Apple Watch pairing process.

After you have finished with this step, it will take some time for your Watch to sync. It should be ready to go and resume functioning once it syncs.

HOW TO FIX THE "UNABLE TO INSTALL UPDATE" ERROR ON AN APPLE WATCH

If the message "Unable to Install Update" appears, there are a few ways to troubleshoot the issue. One way to fix the Apple Watch not checking for updates is to disable the feature that allows you to unlock it with your iPhone. You can also let your Apple Watch receive automatic nightly updates. If your Apple Watch has cellular connectivity, try upgrading the watch straight after turning off Bluetooth and Wi-Fi on your iPhone.

Don't forget to turn the Unlock with iPhone option back on when the Apple Watch has been updated. Another typical error message is "Apple unable to check for update." This section's instructions, which include resetting your Apple Watch and checking your Wi-Fi connection, may also help.

LET YOUR APPLE WATCH UPDATE AUTOMATICALLY OVERNIGHT

There are situations when the update issue can be fixed without your help. If necessary, turn on Automatic Updates in your Apple Watch's settings. Maintain Wi-Fi on your phone and place the Apple Watch close to your iPhone while it is charging. You can activate Apple Watch automatic updates by doing the following:

Get your iPhone's Watch app open.

From the My Watch tab, tap on General.

Select Software Update.

Tap on Automatic Updates.

Verify that Automatic Updates is turned on; the toggle button should be green.

Did you leave it overnight and follow all the update instructions, but your Apple Watch won't update? If you want to finally acquire that Apple Watch software update, try the following troubleshooting procedures!

APPLE WATCH UPDATE REQUIREMENTS

Before updating your watch or using any Apple Watch troubleshooting advice, there are a few actions to follow. For free usage tips for all of your Apple devices, sign up for our Tip of the Day newsletter.

- Make sure your iPhone has the most recent version of iOS installed.
- Charge your Apple Watch at least half way before wearing it. Wi-Fi-connect your iPhone.
- Throughout the upgrade, keep your iPhone close to your Apple Watch.

HOW TO UPDATE APPLE WATCH

Let your watch update automatically throughout the course of the night is one of the best methods to acquire the most recent update. However, you may also manually install the update:

- The Apple Watch Settings app should be opened.
- Press General.
- Then choose Software Update.
- Click Install if you notice that a fresh update is available.
- Follow the instructions on the screen to install it..

Follow the instructions above to determine the Apple Watch software version you are using if you're unsure what the most recent version is. You are using the most recent version if there isn't an update available.

There are several methods to resolve "unable to check for update Apple Watch" issues and troubleshoot Apple Watch updates that won't install updates. Resetting the factory settings on your Apple Watch should be one of your final options.

Scan the QR code to get the free Iphone 14 Manual

CHAPTER SIXTEEN
FEW TWEAKS TO THE SETTINGS

W ith only a few adjustments, you can personalize your smart watch and make it more useful for you.

Having just got a new Apple Watch, but you don't know where to start. Fortunately, using and setting up the Apple Watch is already simple enough. However, a few configuration adjustments might make it even more practical.

You may choose how Siri is activated, which applications display in your dock, whether your apps appear in a list view or a grid, and whether Portrait Mode images from your iPhone serve as your watch's backdrop, among other options. These options and settings will work with any watch that Apple presently offers.

Even additional functions were added to the Apple Watch Series 4 and subsequent models with the WatchOS 9 upgrade, which was released in September 2022.

Additional features include a new app for tracking prescriptions and more thorough sleep monitoring.

The Apple Watch settings you should modify to get the most out of your watch are listed below.

ADJUST ALL OF YOUR ACTIVITY GOALS

Apple provided the capability to modify your objectives for the amount of time you stand and exercise with the introduction of WatchOS 7 in 2020. You could previously just modify your Move (or calories) target.

You may thus modify either one to meet your real daily schedule rather than utilizing the defaults, which are 30 minutes of activity and a total of 12 hours of standing each day.

With this simple adjustment, you'll be able to accomplish your goals when you really begin your day rather than when Apple instructs you to. For instance, you won't feel as if you've missed an hour of time required to shut those rings if you use sleep monitoring overnight and need to charge your watch more often in the morning.

On your watch, launch the Activity app, go to the bottom, and choose Change Goals. Start closing the rings after making your modifications for all three criteria.

SO LONG, RANDOM SCREENSHOTS

You must simultaneously press the side button and Digital Crown on the Apple Watch in order to snap a screenshot. It's an easy and practical method—unless, like me, you regularly activate it by mistake and end up filling the Photos app with random images of your watch face.

Open the Settings app on your watch or the Watch app on your phone, choose General, then scroll down until you find Screenshots. This will completely disable the ability to capture screenshots. For a clean camera roll, choose this option and turn off the Enable Screenshots button next to it.

CUSTOMIZE WHICH APPS APPEAR IN YOUR DOCK

Finding the appropriate applications on your Apple Watch when you need them might be challenging if you have a lot of apps loaded. The Apple Watch's dock is useful in this situation. If you're unfamiliar, the dock is simply an Apple Watch version of the iPhone's app switcher. By clicking the side button, which brings up a carousel of previously used applications, you may activate it.

The dock may be altered to display any applications you like rather than just the most recent ones. Open the Settings menu on your watch, hit Dock, then choose Favorites from the selection that appears. But since you may personalize these applications, I advise doing this through the Phone's Watch app instead.

On your iPhone, launch the Watch app and choose Dock. When you choose the Favorites option, a list of applications is separated into Favorites and Do Not Include parts. The former reveals all of the other applications on your watch that aren't included, while the former just lists the apps that are now in your dock. To edit the Favorites list to your taste, tap the Edit button in the upper right corner.

CHOOSE THE PORTRAIT MODE PHOTOS YOU WANT TO SEE ON YOUR WRIST

Photos taken in Portrait mode may be used as the watch face's backdrop. However, you must first explore the Watch app's settings on your iPhone. Launch the Watch app, then choose the Face Gallery option at the bottom of the screen to get started. Then choose Portraits from the list of New Watch Faces. To choose up to 24 photographs that will rotate when you lift your wrist or touch the screen, pick the Choose Photos option under Content.

KEEP THE APPLE WATCH'S SCREEN AWAKE FOR A LONGER PERIOD OF TIME

You may not always want your Apple Watch's screen to immediately turn off. Maybe you were reading a lengthy text message when you got sidetracked, or maybe you just want to keep an eye on the timer. The Apple Watch's screen normally remains on after a touch for 15 seconds. On your watch, open the Settings app, choose Display & Brightness, and then choose Wake Duration to increase it to 70 seconds. After that, choose Wake for 70 Seconds.

STOP EVERY APP FROM AUTOMATICALLY INSTALLING

If an Apple Watch version of an app exists, it will constantly be installed when you install it on your iPhone. This may soon clog up the app grid on your watch, making it difficult to locate the applications you really want to use.

Go to Settings > General in the Watch app on your phone, then move the switch next to Automatic App Install to the Off position. By entering the Settings menu on the watch, selecting App Store, and turning the switch next to Automatic Downloads, you may also do this on the watch.

By launching the Watch app on your phone and scrolling to the bottom where you can discover a list of accessible applications, you can now install certain apps on your watch individually.

SILENCE THOSE NOISY NOTIFICATIONS

Smart watches might be helpful for covertly glancing at the time or an alert. However, blaring announcements may be counterproductive. By swiping up from the bottom of the screen to open the Control Center, you may activate the quiet mode on your Apple Watch. Then, press the bell-shaped symbol to activate Silent Mode.

Toggle the switch next to Silent Mode in the Sound & Haptics section of the Settings menu on the Apple Watch to enable it. If you'd prefer not to totally silence incoming alerts, there is also a volume slider for regulating how loud or soft they sound.

HAVE SIRI ONLY SPEAK OUT LOUD WHEN YOU'RE WEARING HEADPHONES

When using Siri, you can instantly start exercises, set timers, or check the weather from your watch. However, you may not always want Siri to talk out. Simple settings may be made to limit Siri's auditory feedback to times when you're using headphones. On your Apple Watch, go to the Settings app, choose Siri, and then scroll down to the Siri Responses area. Then choose Headphones Only from the menu. You should now be able to see the name of your Bluetooth headphones above the Siri volume setting on your Apple Watch when it is paired with those headphones.

MAKE TEXT EASIER TO READ BY INCREASING THE FONT SIZE

On a screen this tiny, it might be difficult to see alerts and news headlines. Fortunately, you can boost the text size on the Apple Watch to help your eyes out a little. Launch the Settings application on your watch, choose Display & Brightness, then select Text Size. To change the text size on your watch, rotate the Digital Crown or press the letters that are shown on each side of the meter. Since those watches have larger screens, you'll have additional choices for expanding the text if you own an Apple Watch Series 7, Series 8, or Ultra.

STOP THOSE ANNOYING REMINDERS TO BREATHE

The Breathe reminder is intended to encourage you to take a few minutes to relax and regulate your breathing, which may make you feel more composed and at ease. Take a moment to turn it off so you won't need to be told to breathe, but if you're like me and never do, do it.

On your iPhone, launch the Apple Watch app, then scroll down and touch the mindfulness app link. Select Notifications off next. (Note: If WatchOS 8 is not installed on your watch, this will display as Breathe rather than Mindfulness.)

UNLOCK YOUR APPLE WATCH WITH YOUR IPHONE

There is a less cumbersome method to unlock your Apple Watch without having to type in your password. When your iPhone is unlocked, you may decide to have your Apple Watch unlock automatically.

Enter the Settings section of the Apple Watch by tapping the Digital Crown. Make sure the toggle next to Unlock with iPhone is turned on, then scroll down to Passcode. Every time you do this, your iPhone will now now show a notice stating that it is being used to unlock your Apple Watch.

MAKE IT EASIER TO FIND YOUR APPS

Although the honeycomb app grid is fantastic at first sight, finding the app you want to open might be challenging, especially if you have a lot of applications loaded on your watch. The watch may show all of your applications in an alphabetical list rather than a grid.

Tap App View > List View either in the Settings app on your Watch or in the Watch app on your phone. A list of available applications will now appear when you touch the Digital Crown to exit your watch face. You may easily navigate through this list to find what you're searching for.

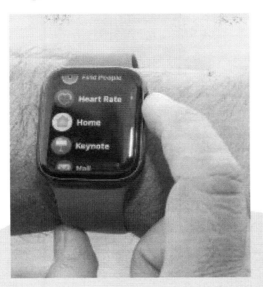

CONTROL WHEN YOU'LL SEE SIRI

There are three methods to make Siri available on your Apple Watch. You may speak by raising your wrist near your lips, holding down the Digital Crown for an extended period of time, or by saying "Hey, Siri."

When I attempt to check the time or read a notice while I'm speaking to someone else (but my watch thinks I'm trying to talk to Siri), I often unintentionally activate Siri. Although it is irritating, it is modifiable.

There are three buttons to regulate when you'll see Siri when you pick Siri in the Watch app on your phone or the Settings app on your Watch. If there are any choices you don't wish to utilize, slide the button to the Off position.

REARRANGE CONTROL CENTER

Similar to Control Center on an iPhone, Control Center on an Apple Watch allows you to rapidly change settings like airplane mode and do not disturb as well as turn on the flashlight.

However, you could discover that the Control Center's default set of choices isn't the greatest match for how you use your watch and that you wish to modify the list. The Bedtime toggle will now be towards the top of the list, which is what it will be for me. So I can swipe up and hit the symbol to monitor my sleep over the weekend when I don't have any specific sleep objectives.

To reach the Control Center on your watch, swipe up from the watch face's bottom. Alternatively, you can slide your finger up to access the Control Center if you're in an app and long-press on the bottom of the screen until you see it start to rise. Anywhere you go, you may use the same method to view your alerts.

By pressing the Edit button at the bottom of the list, you may rearrange the buttons in the Control Center or make some of them invisible. When an option is hidden, an icon will start to wiggle and display a red minus sign. Drag and drag the icons into the position you choose, or press the red minus sign to completely delete a choice.

To return to the watch face after finishing, touch Done or push the Digital Crown on the side of your watch.

HOW TO CREATE CALENDAR EVENTS ON YOUR APPLE WATCH

The ability to create Calendar events straight on your wrist is one of several quality of life enhancements for Apple Watch that were included in watchOS 9 when it was released. Read on to discover how.

The Calendar app for Apple Watch in watchOS 8 and earlier versions only allowed you to browse events you had planned or been invited to for the previous six weeks and the next two years (in List and Day view), but there was no visible method to add an event.

All of that has changed with the release of watchOS 9, as you can now create events directly on your watch and have them synchronized to your iPhone.

METHOD 1

Siri is the first way to create a calendar event on the Apple Watch.

On the Apple Watch, events may be made in two different ways. You may ask Siri to create a calendar event named "lunch with Dad" on October 31 at 1 p.m. by pressing and holding the Digital Crown.

METHOD 2

The Apple Watch's Calendar app is the other method.

- Tap the ellipsis (three dots) button while you are browsing events in the Up Next, Day, or List views.
- Select New Event.
- Include event specifics such the name, description, date, time, and invitees.
- Tap Add after choose which calendar you wish to add the event to.

How to Delete a Calendar Event

Hit the event, choose Delete, and then tap Delete once more to remove a created event. If the event is reoccurring, you may choose to remove only this one or all subsequent ones. Keep in mind that you must use the iPhone's Calendar app in order to modify an event.

HOW TO USE YOUR APPLE WATCH TO SPLIT THE BILL AND CALCULATE TIPS

Every Apple Watch model comes with a built-in calculator software that has a few useful features for calculating how much to tip while dining out and how much everyone in a group should pay if you're sharing the tab.

The two features can be combined, however if you're eating out by yourself, you can simply leave the People option at 1. You can see how it works in the stages below.

Note: You may adjust the calculator layout to replace the TIP button if you see a standard percentage (%) button where it should be. Simply use Tip Function instead of Percent under Settings -> Calculator.

How to Use the Split Bill and Tip Calculator Functions on Apple Watch

- On your Apple Watch, open the Calculator app.
- Enter the bill's total amount.

- Just to the left of the split button in the top-right corner, tap the TIP button.
- To adjust the percentage, use the Digital Crown on your watch while the Tip field is shown in green.
- Tap Persons and then modify the number with the Digital Crown to divide the cost among many people (the maximum is 50).

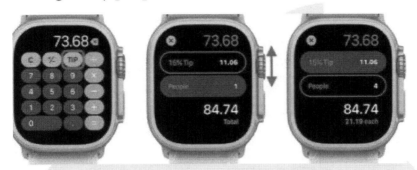

Your tip adjustments will be reflected in the total amount below the two fields, and the amount below that will vary based on the number of persons making payments.

LOST? HOW TO RETRACE YOUR STEPS USING APPLE WATCH'S BACKTRACK

The revised Compass app's Backtrack function lets you track your journey and then assist you in retracing your steps in case you get lost. This feature is available on Apple Watch Ultra, Apple Watch SE, and Apple Watch Series 6 and subsequent devices running watchOS 9.

Backtrack makes a virtual breadcrumb trail of your trip using the GPS on your Apple Watch so you don't have to worry about keeping track of your whereabouts. Apple claims that Backtrack is intended to be used in distant locations, away from familiar locations like your home or place of employment, and outside of heavily populated regions without Wi-Fi, but there is no restriction on where you may use it.

You may utilize watchOS 9's Backtrack function by following these instructions. Be aware that metal watch straps may reduce Backtrack's accuracy.

- The Apple Watch's Compass app should be opened.

- To start recording your path, press the footprints symbol in the bottom-right corner of the screen, then hit Start.

- Scroll down if required, then press Allow Once to give Compass permission to view your most recent locations.

- When you're ready to go back in time, tap Retrace Steps after tapping the stop symbol in the bottom right corner of the screen.

The compass will show your beginning position, and a white arrow will steer you in the appropriate direction as it bounces. Within the compass circle, a white line representing the return route to the beginning location will be visible. To go back to the spot where you initially clicked Backtrack, take the route back.

When you are back where you started, hit the footsteps symbol once again, then choose Delete Steps.

When using Backtrack in conjunction with the Compass app in watchOS 9, you may additionally make Compass Waypoints while you're moving.

HOW TO GET CHARGING REMINDERS AND NOTIFICATIONS FOR APPLE WATCH

The battery life of Apple's most recent Series wristwatch still still guarantees "up to 18 hours" of usage on a single charge, despite the fact that the Apple Watch has been improved every year since it was initially introduced in 2015.

This implies that if you want the Apple Watch to monitor your sleep throughout the night, you must charge it in the evening. It's likely to run out of power if you don't charge it before bed, in which case you'll need to allow it plenty of time in the morning to regain its full charge.

Apple provides a feature that allows you to get reminders to charge your watch before your planned wind down time and then receive notifications on your iPhone when Apple Watch is completely charged to assist you avoid this issue. One automated reminder to charge your watch will sound if it has less than 30% battery an hour before you are supposed to start sleeping. Here is how to activate it:

- Open the Watch app on your iPhone.
- Choosing the My Watch tab.
- Select Sleep by descending the page.
- Turn on the switch next to Charging Reminders under "Battery."

All there is to it is that. If you haven't previously selected Use this Watch for Sleep in the Watch iOS app's Sleep menu, you won't see the Charging Reminders option.

HOW TO USE YOUR APPLE WATCH TO CONTROL YOUR IPHONE

Apple has a feature that lets you manage your iPhone with your Apple Watch in watchOS 9. Read on to see how it works.

Apple unveiled new accessibility capabilities with the introduction of watchOS 9 and iOS 16, including the ability to operate your Apple Watch from your iPhone and vice versa.

However, they may also be helpful if, for instance, your iPhone's screen is broken or unresponsive or the device is just out of reach. Both capabilities are intended to make the Apple Watch and iPhone experience more accessible for those with physical and motor limitations.

You may use your Apple Watch to operate your iPhone by following the instructions below. Keep in mind that the watch must be associated with the iPhone you want to operate, and both the watch and the phone must be running the most recent versions of iOS (watchOS 9 and iOS 16).

Open the Settings app on your Apple Watch.

Tap Accessibility after scrolling down.

Opt for Control Nearby Devices.

From the list, choose your iPhone (or iPad).

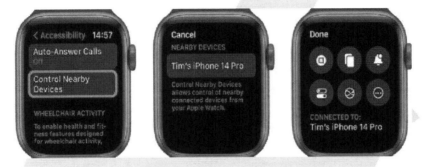

Once you're connected, a set of control buttons will appear that will let you to carry out a number of tasks on your iPhone, including Go to the Home Screen, Open the App Switcher, Open the Notification Center, Open the Control Center, and Activate Siri. The More button also provides options for media playing.

It should be noted that if you control a nearby device when VoiceOver is on on your Apple Watch, VoiceOver will also be activated on that device and you may use the gestures you use on your Apple Watch to control it.

There are many other Apple Watch functions that are interesting to explore. For instance, there are new Pilates and Tai Chi training alternatives, the ECG app may assist detect abnormal heartbeats, and you can even share your own watch faces.

CONCLUSION

You can very well realize that the iPhone-compatible Apple wristwatch is useful, fashionable, and a lot of fun after reading through the details of the Apple Watch in this book, including major Apple Watch features and what an Apple Watch can do using these features, Apple Watch functions, how does an Apple Watch work, and more.

Using Watch-Kit, the software tools it created for third-party app creation, Apple is pushing third-party developers to make applications, specifically for its Apple wristwatch. It is simple to see that there are many other applications for the Apple Watch beyond what it is now capable of.

The Apple watch might soon include capabilities that allow you to use it as an electronic boarding pass, locate your automobile, start your car remotely, and many more services. The claim that smartwatches compromise privacy seems unfounded.

Although it is true that wearable technology gadgets would naturally need connection to the cloud in order to perform at their optimum, this is not a need. Similar to smartphones, smartwatches will include privacy options that let owners choose whatever data they want to send to the cloud or other distant services.

Made in the USA
Las Vegas, NV
27 July 2023

75316404R00087